HEBREWS

Also by Tara-Leigh Cobble

The Bible Recap
The Bible Recap Study Guide
The Bible Recap Journal
The Bible Recap Discussion Guide
The Bible Recap Kids' Devotional
The Bible Recap for Kids
The God Shot
Israel
The Bible Recap 365-Day Chronological Study Bible: English Standard Version

The *Bible Recap* Knowing Jesus Bible Study Series*

Knowing Jesus as King (Matthew)
Knowing Jesus as Servant (Mark)
Knowing Jesus as Savior (Luke)
Knowing Jesus as God (John)

The *Bible Recap* Knowing God Bible Study Series*

Acts
Romans
1 & 2 Corinthians
Galatians & Ephesians
Philippians & Colossians
1 & 2 Thessalonians
1 & 2 Timothy, Titus & Philemon
Hebrews

* General editor

THE BIBLE RECAP **KNOWING GOD SERIES**

HEBREWS

JESUS AS THE FULFILLMENT OF THE OLD TESTAMENT

A 10-WEEK BIBLE STUDY ON THE SUPERIORITY OF CHRIST

TARA-LEIGH COBBLE,

GENERAL EDITOR

WRITTEN BY THE D-GROUP THEOLOGY & CURRICULUM TEAM

BETHANYHOUSE

a division of Baker Publishing Group

Minneapolis, Minnesota

Published by Bethany House Publishers
Minneapolis, Minnesota
BethanyHouse.com

Bethany House Publishers is a division of
Baker Publishing Group, Grand Rapids, Michigan

Printed in the United States of America

Library of Congress Cataloging-in-Publication Data
Names: Cobble, Tara-Leigh editor
Title: Hebrews : Jesus as the fulfillment of the Old Testament : a 10-week Bible study on the superiority of Christ / Tara-Leigh Cobble.
Description: Grand Rapids, Michigan : Bethany House, a division of Baker Publishing Group, [2026] | Series: The Bible recap knowing God series | Includes bibliographical references.
Identifiers: LCCN 2026021388 | ISBN 9780764245916 paperback | ISBN 9781493454136 ebook
Subjects: LCSH: Bible. Hebrews—Study and teaching | Jesus Christ—Person and offices—Biblical teaching
Classification: LCC BS2775.55 .H43 2026
LC record available at https://lccn.loc.gov/2026021388

The D-Group Theology & Curriculum Team is Laura Buchelt, Emily Pickell, Abbey Dane, Kirsten McCloskey, Emma Dotter, Liz Suggs, and Tara-Leigh Cobble.

The general editor is represented by Alive Literary Agency, AliveLiterary.com.

Cover design by Dan Pitts

Baker Publishing Group publications use paper produced from sustainable forestry practices and postconsumer waste whenever possible.

26 27 28 29 30 31 32 7 6 5 4 3 2 1

CONTENTS

HOW TO USE THIS STUDY

While Bible study is vital to the Christian walk, a well-rounded spiritual life comes from engaging with other spiritual disciplines as well. This study is designed not only to equip you with greater knowledge and theological depth, but to help you engage in other formative practices that will create a fuller, more fulfilling relationship with Jesus. We want to see you thrive in every area of your life with God!

Content and Questions

In each of the ten weeks of this study, the teaching and questions are divided into six days, but feel free to do it all at once if that's more manageable for your schedule. If you choose to complete each week's study in one sitting (especially if that time occurs later in the study-week), keep in mind that there are aspects you will want to be mindful of each day: the daily Bible reading, Scripture memorization, and the weekly challenge. Those are best attended to throughout the week.

Daily Bible Reading

The daily Bible reading corresponds to our study. It will take an average of three minutes per day to simply read (not study) the text. If you're an auditory learner, you may prefer to listen to an audio version of these Bible chapters.

Even if you decide to do the week's content and questions in one sitting, we still encourage you to make the daily Bible reading a part of your regular daily rhythm. Establishing a habit of reading the Word every day will help fortify your faith and create greater connection with God.

If you decide to break the study up into the six allotted days each week, your daily Bible reading will align with your study. Days 1–5 will follow our study of Hebrews, Day 6 features a psalm that corresponds to our reading, and Day 7 serves as a catch-up day in case you fall behind.

Scripture Memorization

Memorizing Scripture isn't busywork! It's an important part of hiding God's Word in our hearts (Psalm 119:11). Our memory passage—Hebrews 12:1–11—points to the finished work of Jesus and to God's ongoing work in our lives to conform us to the image of His Son. We encourage you to practice the verses cumulatively—that is, *add* to what you're practicing each week instead of *replacing* it. We quote the English Standard Version (and some of our resources are in that translation as well), but feel free to memorize them in whatever translation you prefer. We suggest working on each week's verse(s) throughout the week, not just at the last minute. We've provided some free tools to help you with this, including a weekly verse song: MyDGroup.org/Hebrews.

Weekly Challenge

This is our practical response to what we've learned each week. We want to be "doers of the word, and not hearers only" (James 1:22). You'll find a variety of challenges, and we encourage you to lean into them all—especially the ones you find *most* challenging! This will help strengthen your spiritual muscles and encourage you in your faith. As with the memory verse, you'll want to begin this practice earlier in the week, especially because some weekly challenges include things to do each day of the week (e.g., prayers, journaling, etc.).

Resources

This is a Scripture-heavy study, and you'll find yourself looking up passages often. If you're new to studying Scripture, this will be a great way to dig in and sharpen your skills! You will feel more equipped and less intimidated as you move through each chapter. Some questions may ask you to refer to a Bible dictionary, commentary, or Greek or Hebrew lexicon, but you don't need to purchase those tools. There are lots of free options available online. We've linked to some of our favorite tools—plus additional resources such as podcasts, articles, and apps—at MyDGroup.org/Hebrews.

Groups

Because each week has a lot of questions in the content, we offer the following recommendation for those who plan to discuss the study in a weekly group meeting. As each member is doing their homework, we suggest they mark their favorite items with a star and mark any confusing items with a question mark. This serves as preparation for the group discussion and helps direct the conversation in beneficial ways. Group leaders, please note the starred prompt(s) in each chapter; we've highlighted these for you as topics you may find helpful to prioritize in group discussions.

INTRODUCTION

Hebrews is a general term that refers to the Israelites or the descendants of Abraham. The book of Hebrews has no named author or recipients. However, much of it relates to Israel's history, and the author points to Jesus as the ultimate fulfillment of the Jewish faith, which is how the book came to be known as Hebrews.

Scholars tend to agree that the book was written to a group of Hebrews—or Jews—most of whom had believed in Jesus as the promised and prophesied Savior. It was likely written in AD 67–69, because it mentions Timothy's release from prison, the increased persecution of believers (likely at the hand of Nero), and Levitical practices specific to the time.

As for the possible author, scholars have suggested Paul, Barnabas, Apollos, Luke, Philip, Aquila, and Clement of Rome. Based on the tone of the letter, it's likely not Paul. A helpful perspective—and the one we'll proceed with in this study—is to embrace the anonymity of the human writer and entrust credit for authorship to the Holy Spirit. While we don't know who wrote it or who it was originally written to, we can have confidence that the apostles and early church leaders viewed this as Scripture. So while we don't have as much background information as we do with most other books of the Bible, we have everything we need to study Hebrews as God's Word.

This book's main theme is the superiority of Christ. Arguing logically, the author compares the law and the old covenant with Christ and the new covenant. It's possible that new Hebrew believers were tempted to return to their Jewish faith because of the intense persecution of Christians. In the face of this, the author showed how following Jesus was not a break from their Jewish roots, but a fulfillment of everything they had been promised! The writer wasn't comparing an old evil with a new good; he was comparing an old *good* with a new *better*.

While reading the book of Hebrews, you may find it helpful to keep a bookmark in the Old Testament, particularly the book of Leviticus. The better you understand the Levitical priesthood, the tabernacle, systems of offerings and feasts, and God's provision for nearness with His people, the better you will understand Hebrews.

Covenant, which is simply a sincere and devout promise, is another key concept in Hebrews. In the Old Testament, God made covenants with many different people. Some of them were conditional—requiring human obedience—and some of them were unconditional—requiring only God's faithfulness.

If at any point you find yourself confused while studying this dense, rich book, zoom out and remember this: The author is showing how *Jesus is better*.

WEEK 1

Hebrews 1–2

Scripture to Memorize

Since we are surrounded by so great a cloud of witnesses, let us also lay aside every weight, and sin which clings so closely, and let us run with endurance the race that is set before us . . .

Hebrews 12:1

Note: If you haven't yet read How to Use This Study on page 7, please do that before continuing. It will provide you with a proper framework and helpful tools.

DAILY BIBLE READING

Day 1: Hebrews 1:1–4
Day 2: Hebrews 1:5–14
Day 3: Hebrews 2:1–4
Day 4: Hebrews 2:5–13
Day 5: Hebrews 2:14–18
Day 6: Psalm 102
Day 7: Catch-Up Day

Corresponds to Day 355 of *The Bible Recap.*

WEEKLY CHALLENGE

See page 35 for more information.

DAY 1

Hebrews 1:1–4

READ HEBREWS 1:1–4

The author of Hebrews cut to the chase, jumping right into the theme of his letter. The first four verses lay the groundwork for the thirteen chapters that follow. Simply put, Jesus is better and greater. In today's passage, we see that He's greater than any other authority in all of creation.

Review 1:1.

1. Who was the ultimate author of Hebrews? (See the introduction to this study for help.)

   A. Paul
   B. Apollos
   C. The Holy Spirit
   D. Priscilla
   E. Barnabas

Regardless of who God used as His mouthpiece, He's always been the true Holy Ghost–writer of all Scripture.

The author's reference to "our fathers by the prophets" would've deeply resonated with his Jewish audience. The "fathers" were the patriarchs—the founders of the Hebrew nation—Abraham, Isaac, and Jacob. And the prophets were the people who spoke on behalf of God in the Old Testament, testifying about a coming Messiah. The prophets included Moses, Elijah, and Isaiah—to name only a few.

These two groups, the patriarchs and the prophets, were held in high esteem among faithful Jews. Thus the conjunction that opens 1:2 ("but") serves as an important hinge point.

Review 1:2a.

2. Fill in the blanks below.

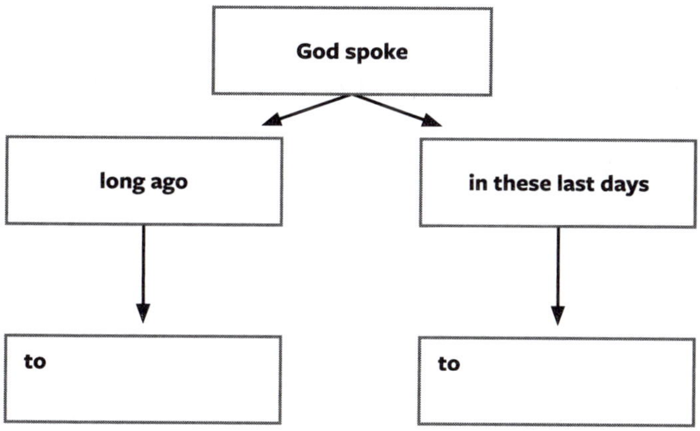

3. How did God's method of communication with us in the "these last days" shift from how He communicated in the days "long ago"?

"In these last days" is the time period since Jesus the Messiah was raised from the dead and ascended to heaven. Since then, believers have been and will be in these last days until He returns.

Review 1:2b–3.

As our study progresses, we'll learn more about what the Son does; but first, it's crucial that we understand who the Son is.

★ 4. What six truths did the author establish about the Son? **Using a Bible study tool, fill in the truths about Jesus.** In the last column, describe this trait in your own words. Two are provided for you.

Truths About the Son	Significance	In Your Own Words
Heir of all things	As God's Son, Jesus was given all authority.	God put everything in Jesus's hands.
	He was present and active in the creation of all things.	
He is the radiance of God's glory and exact imprint of His nature	Jesus perfectly reflects God.	Looking at Jesus is like looking at a picture of God.
	He sustains all of creation.	
	He made a way for us to be saved.	
	Because He is divine, He is seated in heaven in a place of honor.	

The third characteristic on the list may be the hardest to comprehend.

Many have used a stamp to illustrate this—Jesus is a "stamp" of God on earth. Or they've described Jesus as the visible beam of God's light shining on us. In his letter to the Colossians, Paul described Jesus as "the image of the invisible God" (Colossians 1:15), and we see that idea repeated here.

But perhaps nobody explains it more clearly and more plainly than Jesus Himself.

5. Write John 14:9 below.

So why is Jesus better than anything and anyone in all of creation? Because He *is* the creator!

Did you notice what action Jesus took after He made purification for our sins? He sat down. Why? Because the work was finished. For the original audience, this positioning might bring to mind the court of the Sanhedrin (the Jewish religious leaders). This ancient court had two scribes: the one on the left wrote convictions and punishments, and the one on the right wrote acquittals. How fitting that the Son of God is seated in the place representing our pardon.[1] The author reiterated this encouraging truth throughout the letter.

Review 1:4.

Discussing Jesus's hierarchy above the angels might seem to be an arbitrary detail here. But throughout Hebrews, the writer called his audience back to a better way. If Jews at this time held their "fathers and the prophets" in high regard, then it's possible they held the angels even higher.

6. Read Acts 7:53. What was one role the angels played in Old Testament history?

While the angels' contribution to the Jewish faith was significant, they could hardly compare to the majesty of the Son of God. We'll dive deeper into this topic tomorrow.

DAY 2

Hebrews 1:5–14

READ HEBREWS 1:5–14

Knowing the cultural and spiritual heritage of his audience, the writer of Hebrews provided a number of Old Testament excerpts to ensure they developed a proper view of angels.

It's important to note that the original authors of each quoted text, perhaps unknowingly, spoke of two prophecies being fulfilled: one in the near future and another in a more distant future. As we examine each quote, this process may feel repetitive, but be intentional as you read. Look for things that may be new information for you.

As you read, take notice of how the text highlights the superiority of Jesus over angels. These Old Testament passages pointed to Jesus's divinity and to Jesus as the only one to be worshiped.

Review 1:5a.

Old Testament Excerpt #1: Psalm 2:7
Author: Widely believed to be King David
Original intent: Celebrated the earthly king anointed by God
Ultimate fulfillment: God speaking of His Son, Jesus

1. Who does the Hebrews writer say did *not* receive this distinction of sonship?

Review 1:5b.

Old Testament Excerpt #2: 2 Samuel 7:14

Author: The prophet Nathan

Original intent: Assured King David that his offspring would be on the throne

Ultimate fulfillment: The Messiah came from the seed of David

Review 1:6.

Old Testament Excerpt #3: Deuteronomy 32:43

Author: Moses

Original intent: A worshipful song about Yahweh, the one true God

Ultimate fulfillment: The angels still worship Yahweh, who is Jesus

2. Who did the Hebrews writer establish as all of creation's rightful object of worship?

Review 1:7.

Old Testament Excerpt #4: Psalm 104:4

Author: Unknown, but widely believed to be David

Original intent: Establishing God's authority over the angels

Ultimate fulfillment: Jesus holds this same place of authority over the angels

Review 1:8–9.

Old Testament Excerpt #5: Psalm 45:6–7

Author: The Sons of Korah

Original intent: Recognition of God's everlasting kingdom of righteousness

Ultimate fulfillment: Announces the deity of Jesus and His everlasting kingdom

3. Take a closer look at the Hebrews writer's words in 1:8. Who was calling the Son "God"?

Review 1:10–12.

Old Testament Excerpt #6: Psalm 102:25–27

Author: Unknown

Original intent: Recognizing God as the creator, who is unchanging and unending

Ultimate fulfillment: Jesus is the unchanging, unending king

Review 1:13.

Old Testament Excerpt #7: Psalm 110:1

Author: King David

Original intent: A promise of honor and victory for King David

Ultimate fulfillment: Jesus holds the victory and honor over all creation

4. Who did the Hebrews writer say was *not* given this place of honor?

Review 1:14.

★ 5. What is the role of angels?

The author used these proof texts to help his audience understand the key truth that Jesus is superior to angels.

As modern readers, we may wonder why so much real estate was given to this topic. You likely didn't begin this study with an inordinate reverence for angels. But just like the Jews who originally received this letter, humans have a tendency to put someone or something on a pedestal. Often, these can be good, healthy things. But also like the original audience, we must be reminded over and over that Jesus is better.

★ 6. Ask God to reveal anything in your life that has been elevated above a love for Christ. If anything comes to mind that has taken more of your time and attention than serving Christ, write it below and ask God to correct your disordered desires.

DAY 3

Hebrews 2:1–4

READ HEBREWS 2:1–4

If you've been to the beach and played in the ocean, you know how easily drifting can happen. Within minutes, you look up from freely bobbing in the waves to find you're much farther from land than you intended. Drifting away didn't take effort—it just took distraction. This is exactly what the writer of Hebrews warned his audience about in today's passage.

Review 2:1.

Therefore is a connecting word that prompts us to look back and consider what we've just learned. It typically indicates the place where information meets application.

1. What did the writer call his audience to do? What was his warning if they didn't take heed?

In Hebrews 1, the writer went to great lengths to prove through the Holy Scriptures that Jesus wasn't some crazed street preacher. He wasn't even *just* better than the angels. The author proved to them that Jesus is the everlasting Son of God, the creator of all things, and the Messiah they'd longed for.

And this is where the rubber meets the road: We can't unhear this truth about Jesus, and our lives should reflect it.

Review 2:2.

As we'll see many times in this letter, the writer referred to something here that most of his Jewish audience would've immediately understood.

★ 2. What message did the angels deliver to the patriarchs and the prophets? (Hint: Look back at Day 1's sixth prompt.)

★ 3. Read Romans 3:20. What did the law bring knowledge of?

God's laws were a reliable guide for holy living, but what the law could not do was provide salvation for souls (more on this in Hebrews 8).

Review 2:3.

Here, it's crucial that we pause. We mustn't carelessly skip over—or dangerously assume understanding of—what the writer means by "this great salvation."

The apostle Paul gave one of the simplest, most succinct gospel presentations in a letter to the Corinthians.

4. To better understand the correlation between the gospel and salvation, read 1 Corinthians 15:1–4 and complete the chart below.

Christ ________	**for**	**our** ________
Christ	**was**	________
Christ	**was**	________

This is the great story of our salvation. All humankind is born in sin, and we cannot save ourselves. But through an act of sheer love and grace, Christ took on our sin, died for us, and was raised from the dead, rescuing us from total destruction both now and in eternity. In short, Jesus is better than the law because Jesus is able to save completely (more on this in Hebrews 7).

But the writer's warning also stands: If this great salvation is neglected, there is no plan B. There is no escape from the wrath of God through good works or keeping the law. Jesus fulfilled the law. He is the only option for salvation (see John 14:6 and Acts 4:10; more on this in Hebrews 10).

★ 5. Why is it easy or natural to let our hearts drift away from such good news?

D. A. Carson described the human condition well when he wrote,

> People do not drift toward holiness. Apart from grace-driven effort, people do not gravitate toward godliness, prayer, obedience to Scripture, faith, and delight in the Lord. We drift toward compromise and call it tolerance; we drift toward disobedience and call it freedom; we drift toward superstition and call it faith. We cherish the indiscipline of lost self-control and call it relaxation; we slouch toward prayerlessness and delude ourselves into thinking we have escaped legalism; we slide toward godlessness and convince ourselves we have been liberated.[1]

However, make no mistake, drifting is *not* about slipping out of the hands of God and losing your salvation. The writer warned that drifting away from God's best would lead us into dangerous waters and even into the discipline of the Lord. But never out of His hands (John 10:28).

Review 2:4.

6. In addition to those who shared the good news of Jesus and His eternal salvation by word of mouth, what four ways did God communicate His salvation to humankind?

As we learned on Day 1, God spoke to our fathers many times and in many ways—but now, He has spoken to us. Let us not drift from what we have heard.

DAY 4

Hebrews 2:5–13

READ HEBREWS 2:5–13

Review 2:5–8.

In 2:5, the writer hinted at a coming kingdom—"the world to come"—and once again confirmed that angels will not be in charge when this new world is established.

Pointing to Psalm 8:4–6, the writer asked a logical question. He looked around at humanity and essentially said, *"Us? You want to put* us *in charge?"*

1. What three things describe humanity in 2:7–8?

Shocking though it may be, this wasn't a new idea. This plan goes back to the beginning of time. Since creation, the earth has been subject to man (Genesis 1:26).

As the writer noted in 2:8, when we look at the world around us, we hardly feel like we're in control of what's happening. We see death, chaos, and pain, so how could "everything" possibly be in subjection to man? What—or who—is the missing piece?

Review 2:9.

The writer revealed that through one Man—Jesus—this prophecy will be fulfilled. This "world to come" pointed to the new creation—the kingdom in which Jesus will rule and be crowned with glory and honor.

We've already seen the supremacy and deity of Christ—that He is far above the angels. Now we see the *humanity* of Christ—that He was made a little lower than the angels. Fully God. Fully man. Both were necessary to rescue humankind from death.

Before we continue, it's important that we debunk a myth. Some argue that this verse says Jesus was a *created* being—that He was *made*. The Bible tells a much different story.

2. Fill in the blanks in the following passages.

"All things were __________ through him, and without him was not any thing ________ that was ________."—John 1:3

"For by him [Jesus] all things were ____________."—Colossians 1:16

"...through whom also he [Jesus] ___________ the world."—Hebrews 1:2

3. Did you know that Jesus was the active agent in the creation of all things? How does this change or enrich your view of His role in the Trinity?

Hebrews 2:9 contains another confusing phrase: "was made *lower than the angels*" (emphasis added). Some scholars say this is a geographical distinction (earth is lower than heaven), others say it is a spiritual distinction

(He took on a body that could die, whereas angels cannot die), and others say it is a temporary status.

All humans are made in the image of God—a distinction angels do not have (Genesis 1:27; 1 Peter 1:12). And all believers (children of God) will one day reign with Christ over all creation, including angels (1 Corinthians 6:3; 2 Timothy 2:12; Revelation 3:21). In the meantime, angels serve God's children as His ministers (Hebrews 1:7, 14). And Jesus, in His humility, took on flesh in order to save and serve us.

Review 2:10.

Because of sin, man could not be crowned with glory and honor. But through Jesus, God made it possible for many sons and daughters to be brought to glory in His coming kingdom.

The word *perfect* carries a richer meaning than it might appear to. It comes from the word *teleioō*, which means "to complete" or "to accomplish" in the way you would accomplish or fulfill a task.[1] Jesus wasn't "made perfect"—He was always perfect. When He came to earth to suffer as a man, He completed the task of securing our salvation once for all time (John 19:28–30).

Review 2:11–13.

4. **Read 2:11 in the New Living Translation (NLT).** How does this translation clarify why Jesus would refer to us as His brothers and sisters?

Again, using a series of Old Testament proof texts from Psalms and Isaiah, the writer identified man as being of the same family as Jesus. Jesus calls us His "brothers and sisters" and God's children. By using these Old Testament texts, the writer showed his audience that Jesus is the fulfillment of the Old Testament. This truth is consistent with the teachings of Jesus Himself (John 5:39). This is the theme of Hebrews: In every book, and in every chapter, the Bible is pointing us to Jesus.

DAY 5

Hebrews 2:14–18

READ HEBREWS 2:14–18

Yesterday, we learned why Jesus is qualified to be our final sacrifice—how both the Old Testament and the New Testament point to His deity *and* humanity. Today, we get a peek into the heart of Jesus and why He was willing to go through such suffering for our sake.

Review 2:14–15.

1. What two things did Jesus deliver us from by becoming like us, taking on flesh?

We tend to think of death as simply the end of life, but when sin entered the world, death cast a shadow on all of creation. Sin and death have fractured our existence in such a way that anxiety, pain, fear, and worry threaten to be the drumbeat of our daily lives.

But Jesus became a man not only to defeat death but also to demolish the power that the fear of death held over us. Jesus's deliverance wasn't just for our eternal rescue; it also gave us the chance to reengage with the abundant life He promised us (John 10:10).

★ 2. Does Jesus's deliverance change the way you think about death? Does it change the way you think about daily life? Explain.

Did you notice the great paradox of Jesus's rescue plan? He used death to defeat death. How fitting that Jesus would beat Satan at his own game, ultimately rendering him powerless. While Satan is allowed temporary, limited power, it falls under the realm of God's sovereignty. Essentially, Satan is on a leash and his time is short. God has always held the ultimate power of life and death.

Review 2:16–17.

This term *the seed of Abraham* (2:16 KJV) would've deeply resonated with a Jewish audience. They recognized that the lineage of Abraham (i.e., Israel) was God's chosen people. But through Christ, God's salvation was extended to all nations, just like God had planned all along (Galatians 3:8). It's worth noting that the writer of Hebrews did not refer to the seed of Adam here, which would have been a reference to all humanity. God's deliverance from slavery is available only to those who believe in Jesus.

3. How did the writer describe the type of high priest Jesus is?

We'll learn more about the role of the high priest in the days to come, but in short, the high priest, according to the Jewish laws, interceded on behalf of the nation of Israel. Once a year, he followed a strict protocol to enter God's presence and made atonement for the sins of all the people.

4. Look up the term *atonement*, or *propitiation*, in a Bible dictionary. Define it in your own words below.

When Jesus died for our sins, He became our great high priest, offering ultimate forgiveness for the sins of all who come to Him. But Jesus didn't complete this task from a distance. He came to earth, experienced life as a human, and endured all the temptations and pain we experience every day.

Review 2:18.

Here we see the character, love, mercy, and grace of Jesus on display. As believers, we know Jesus suffered when He died on the cross. But we may fail to remember that He also suffered through temptation. He never sinned, but because He became human, He understands our struggle.

The next time you want to hide from God because of your temptation and failures, remember that Jesus is a Savior who *gets it*. He literally died so that you wouldn't try to hide from Him. He left heaven, came to earth, suffered through temptation, died on a cross, and then defeated death in order that we might *know* that He's where the joy is!

5. What stood out to you most in this week's study? Why?

6. What did you learn or relearn about God and His character this week?

DAY 6

Corresponding Psalm & Prayer

READ PSALM 102

1. What correlation do you see between Psalm 102 and this week's study?

2. What portions of this psalm stand out to you most?

3. Close by praying this prayer aloud:

Father,

You are enthroned forever; You are remembered throughout all generations! Jesus, You are the radiance of the glory of the Father and the exact imprint of His nature. Spirit, thousands of years ago, You led the psalmist and the writer of Hebrews to record these beautiful truths, and You guide us in understanding them now.

Lord, You're merciful and faithful, but I'm forgetful and prideful. I was a prisoner, doomed to die, and Your Son set me free. But sometimes I act like my own righteous works will save me instead of acknowledging His works have saved me. Jesus sits at Your right hand because His sacrifice is complete, but I treat His finished work as if it isn't sufficient—for me or for others. I've put myself in charge. I've tried to condemn those who You've already pardoned. And I repent, God.

Like the Hebrews, I can drift so easily. Will You give me grace-driven effort? Will You guide me toward holiness? Will You make me Your servant who dwells securely so that I might enjoy Your love forever?

You're better than the angels and every created thing. May my life reflect that reality. I surrender my life to You, Lord—every moment of my day, each decision I make, I yield my will and way to Your perfect will and way.

I love You too. Amen.

DAY 7

Rest, Catch Up, or Dig Deeper

WEEKLY CHALLENGE

On Day 3, the writer of Hebrews warned his readers against one of the greatest dangers of the Christian faith: drifting away from the truth we have heard (see Hebrews 2:1).

Perhaps the tenet of our faith many of us are most prone to drift from is grace. In fact, when the apostle Paul warned against falling from grace (see Galatians 5:4), it was a warning against falling into self-righteousness.

Grace is when you get something you don't deserve. And our salvation is perhaps the best example of the grace God has extended to us.

When we doubt God's willingness to extend us His grace for salvation, we run toward works-based righteousness. When we doubt God's willingness to keep us by His grace, we run toward performance and mask wearing.

To avoid drifting from grace this week, set a daily alarm or reminder in your phone or calendar as a prompt. When you see the reminder, spend one minute in prayer centered around God's grace for you—that you would see it, remember it, and live out of it.

WEEK 2

Hebrews 3–4

Scripture to Memorize

. . . looking to Jesus, the founder and perfecter of our faith, who for the joy that was set before him endured the cross, despising the shame, and is seated at the right hand of the throne of God.

Hebrews 12:2

DAILY BIBLE READING

Day 1: Hebrews 3:1–6

Day 2: Hebrews 3:7–14

Day 3: Hebrews 3:15–19

Day 4: Hebrews 4:1–13

Day 5: Hebrews 4:14–16

Day 6: Psalm 95

Day 7: Catch-Up Day

Corresponds to Day 355 of *The Bible Recap*.

WEEKLY CHALLENGE

See page 58 for more information.

DAY 1

Hebrews 3:1–6

READ HEBREWS 3:1–6

Review 3:1.

1. What word does today's reading start with?

   A. Therefore
   B. Forget
   C. Regardless
   D. Instead
   E. For

The writer of Hebrews wasn't changing topics here. This connecting word lets us know that he was elaborating on what he'd already said.

★ 2. Look back at last week's study. Then list a few of the author's main points from the first two chapters of Hebrews.

What were faithful brothers and sisters in Christ supposed to do in response to these truths? They were to consider Christ—to think about Jesus, meditate on truth, and regularly remind themselves of who He is. Jesus is an *apostle* (He was sent by God), and He is the ultimate *high priest* (He represents people before God).

Review 3:2–4.

To the Jews who read this letter, Moses was more than just a leader. He received the law from God on their behalf. As one of the most revered prophets, his job was to lead and serve God's people; he guided them to live as God commanded (Exodus 33:12–17; Numbers 12:7). He wasn't perfect, but he was faithful. The author of Hebrews honored Moses while showing his Jewish audience how much greater Jesus is.

The word *house* referred to the people of God. While the punctuation wasn't original to the text, the parentheses in 3:4 show English readers that the author was making a clarifying point: Every house has a builder. These verses describe Christ's unique participation in God's work. Jesus isn't a servant in the house, like Moses—the house exists because of Him.

Review 3:5–6a.

3. Fill in the table below.

Name	Location	Role
Moses	In	
Jesus		Son

The Greek word translated *servant* (therapōn) is unique. It refers to an honored, willing attendant who serves closely and faithfully. In the New Testament, this term is used only to describe Moses, highlighting his unique dignity and nearness to God. But Moses's faithfulness pointed forward to an even greater servant leader: Jesus Christ.

4. Write Mark 10:45 below.

Review 3:6b.

God's people don't earn their salvation. Salvation is a gift that comes through faith in Jesus, and it can't be taken away. If you've placed your faith in Jesus, your salvation is secure (Romans 10:9–10; 1 John 5:11–13). Placing your faith in Jesus means more than believing He existed or was a good teacher. Faith in Him is a faith that says, "I could never earn my own righteousness in God's eyes, but I trust in Jesus's life of perfect works (not my own), His sacrificial death that paid my sin debt, and His bodily resurrection from the grave. He is the only way to the Father's house" (see John 14:6).

Lives marked by trust in Jesus testify to what He has already done, is doing, and will do. Among many other things, He paid for our sin. He is our confidence. He gives us hope. And He covers our shortcomings as we boast in Him. Jesus saved us, gave us His Spirit, and *is coming back* (Philippians 1:6; Acts 1:11; John 15:26).

★ 5. In what ways or at what times are you tempted to place confidence in yourself? How could you redirect your confidence back to Jesus—His death, resurrection, and return?

DAY 2

Hebrews 3:7–14

READ HEBREWS 3:7–14

Review 3:7–9.

The writer of Hebrews quoted Psalm 95—a passage the original audience was very familiar with. In contrast to Christ's faithfulness, Psalm 95 describes Israel's unbelief in the wilderness. After God rescued Israel out of slavery in Egypt, He led them through the wilderness—a journey meant to teach them to trust His care and follow His lead (Exodus 7–12, 14; Deuteronomy 8:2–3). Instead of leaning in and learning to trust God, Israel often pushed back, complaining, doubting, and testing God.

The author reminded his audience that the Holy Spirit isn't *solely* the author of past revelation, like in the story in Psalm 95. According to 3:7, "the Holy Spirit says"—not "the Holy Spirit *said*." God is still speaking through His Word right now! The command "Do not harden your hearts" warns against the deliberate, willful unbelief that marked Israel in the wilderness. What was dangerous for Israel is dangerous today.

In Scripture, the heart represents the whole person—mind, will, and emotions—so this is a call to stay responsive and obedient to God's voice in all areas of life. Even though Israel saw God's power and grace for forty years, they repeatedly rejected Him. The author of Hebrews applied this case study to his readers: God's grace should lead to faith and endurance.

★ 1. How have you seen God's grace lead to faith and endurance in your own life? (Note: Look back at the weekly challenge from last week if you need a reminder of the definition of *grace*.)

Review 3:10–11.

God's wrath is not impulsive or out of control. It's a righteous reaction to persistent disobedience. His statement "They shall not enter my rest" comes from Psalm 95, which reflects on Israel's rebellion in Numbers 14. Because Israel rejected God's command to enter the land, they didn't experience His rest. This warning is timeless: Those who refuse to believe, like Israel, will miss God's promised rest.

Under the old covenant, blessings like daily rest—or peace—were dependent on the obedience of God's people (Deuteronomy 28). So in Psalm 95, *rest* meant obeying God's command to enter the promised land (and therefore life in a new home after years of being enslaved). Hebrews teaches that new covenant rest includes spiritual *and* eternal realities. Those who've placed their faith in Jesus, and choose to actively depend on Him, can experience His rest in their daily lives. But believers are also *guaranteed* eternal rest (salvation) through Christ (Romans 10:9–10).

Review 3:12–14.

Unbelief isn't simply doubt or questioning; it's a willful refusal to trust God that leads to spiritual rebellion. The verb *apostēnai* ("to fall away" or "turn away") literally means "to depart or rebel." Here, it doesn't describe casual drifting or a moment of questioning. It's a deliberate departure from faith.

2. What did the writer call his audience?

3. Summarize 1 John 2:19–21.

Perseverance is a community project. The command to "encourage one another daily" (3:13 NIV) is about guarding against the appearance of faith that hardens into unbelief. Fake faith always falls short. True believers can't lose their salvation, but they can become trapped in sin more easily when they live isolated lives, lacking regular encouragement from other believers.

Think about dirty dishes slowly piling up in a kitchen sink. Over time, those dirty dishes begin to smell and attract flies. In a similar way, being hardened is a process in which sinful choices or thoughts that might seem insignificant build up, causing catastrophic problems (James 1:14–15).

Sin doesn't announce itself as rebellion—it deceives slowly, numbing the heart until unbelief and disobedience feel normal. Encouragement and accountability are God's design to keep His people sensitive to truth and resistant to the enemy's lies.

★ 4. What lies are you believing that lead you to minimize your sin or doubt God's truth? Write them on the dirty dishes below.

Today signals a present opportunity to respond in faith—and that's good news. God is faithful and just: He responded to the Hebrews with forgiveness, and He responds to us with forgiveness (1 John 2:12).

The phrase *have become* shows that the Hebrew believers had an established and ongoing relationship with God. And it's important to note that 3:14 isn't about earning or keeping salvation. It's a charge to live out a fellowship with Christ that already exists through genuine faith. Perseverance doesn't *create* salvation; it *proves* it.

★ 5. Think about someone you know who's persevered in a way that evidenced their faith. Describe what you've seen in them.

DAY 3

Hebrews 3:15–19

READ HEBREWS 3:15–19

Review 3:15–18.

The author of Hebrews just couldn't get enough of Psalm 95! Quoting it again, he presented a renewed call: The danger of hardening our hearts is present for *every* generation. The "today" of God's grace still stands, but it will not last forever. Every person will have to face God at the end of their life or when Christ returns.

Through a series of rhetorical questions, the writer reminded his audience of stories they knew well.

1. Fill in the table below.

Rhetorical Question	Cross-Reference(s)	Implied Answer
For who were those who heard and yet rebelled?	Exodus 14:11–12; Numbers 14:1–4; Deuteronomy 1:26–33	Israel rebelled. God told them to enter the promised land and they said, *"Let's go back to Egypt!"*
	Numbers 14:22	Yes, it was. They saw God's glory through the plagues, Passover, and parting of the Red Sea, yet they still rebelled.

And with whom was he provoked for forty years?	Numbers 14:22–23, 33	
	Deuteronomy 2:14–15; Numbers 14:29–30; 26:64–65	Yes, it was. The generation that rebelled in the wilderness died in the wilderness (with the exception of Joshua and Caleb).
And to whom did he swear that they would not enter his rest, but to those who were disobedient?	Deuteronomy 1:34–35	

2. Read Numbers 13:25–33 and 14:5–10. What was the difference between Joshua and Caleb and the rest of Israel?

Review 3:18 again.

Here, the author identified the ultimate reason the Israelites were forbidden from entering God's rest in the promised land: *disobedience*. This word (*apeitheō*) highlights not just disbelief in the mind but willful rebellion expressed through action. The author showed that unbelief always expresses itself in disobedience. Faith and obedience are inseparable in God's economy.

★ 3. Describe a time when your faith in Jesus motivated or empowered you to obey despite temptation to disobey.

Review 3:19.

Israel's failure to enter wasn't solely circumstantial. It was spiritual. A lack of belief was the reason for their disobedience. The author's "so we see" signaled this central truth: Unbelief shuts people out of God's rest, just as faith alone opens the way into His rest (Ephesians 2:8–9).

★ 4. Review your study of 3:6b from Week 2, Day 1. In your own words, what is the gospel, the good news of Jesus?

DAY 4

Hebrews 4:1–13

READ HEBREWS 4:1–13

Review 4:1.

After reminding the Hebrew audience that the promise of the gospel is still available, the author gave a strong warning: "Let us fear." But this fear isn't like anxiety or worry. It's a reverent awareness that God's promises are real. The author was prompting his audience to recall Israel's story: They heard God's instruction but didn't believe Him, and they missed out on His rest.

The writer was basically saying, *"Hey, Hebrews? Don't let that be you. Stay responsive to God, take Him seriously, and lean in with faith. And remember, this isn't about losing your salvation. It's about not growing numb to the gospel you've already received."* Even after Israel's failure, God's promise remains open. His invitation to enter His rest still stands for everyone who hears His voice and believes.

1. Have you received the free gift of salvation through Jesus? If so, briefly summarize the story of your salvation.

2. Review Week 2, Day 2. What are the two types of new covenant rest?

Review 4:2–3.

The writer wanted the Hebrews to understand the contrast between Israel's unbelief and those who respond to God in faith; those who believe enter His rest—not just one day in the future, but right now. The work God required has already been finished. Jesus's victory was secured outside of time (Revelation 13:8; 1 Peter 1:19–20). So the invitation is the same as it's always been: Hear God's Word, trust Him, and step into the rest He's *already* provided and is still providing.

3. Look up the following verses and note what they indicate about time, believers, or Jesus.

John 8:58	Jesus existed long before Abraham.
Colossians 1:16–17	
1 Peter 1:19–20	
Revelation 13:8	
Revelation 22:13	

Review 4:4–7.

Anchoring this invitation in the creation story (God rested on the seventh day, and that rest has been available ever since), the writer returned to Psalm 95. God's rest has always been available, but unbelief still keeps people out.

Psalm 95 says "today" for a reason: Every generation gets the same invitation to trust God while there's still time. Hearing and even agreeing with the truth is pointless without actually believing it and being changed by it.

Review 4:8.

Because Joshua led Israel into the land after their rebellion in the wilderness, was *that* the rest God promised? The author says *no*—if Joshua had led Israel to genuine rest, God wouldn't have been talking about another day through David. Joshua offered a temporary, physical rest, but Jesus offers true and lasting rest. Joshua brought God's people into the land, but only Jesus can bring us into God's presence!

Review 4:9–10.

There's still a "Sabbath rest" available for God's people—a rest that isn't about land but about relationship. It's God's own rest, the kind He enjoyed when His work was finished (Genesis 2). And because of Jesus, we get to enter that rest too. We stop striving to earn what He's already secured, and we learn to rest in His finished work instead of our own.

4. Has there been a time when your Christian service or church activities resulted in busyness rather than connection with (or closeness to) God? If so, briefly describe.

Review 4:11.

When we "make every effort" (NIV) to enter God's rest, that's not to say we *earn* it. Instead, this verse points to actively holding on to it through faith. It's a paradox of learning to rest in what Jesus has *already* finished instead of slipping back into self-reliance. Here, the author pointed the Hebrews to the Israelites again as a warning: The same drift that occurred in Israel can occur in us if we're not careful. So we stay diligent—showing up, encouraging one another, depending on the Spirit, and choosing to trust Christ instead of ourselves.

★ 5. What makes it hardest for you to rest in what Jesus has already finished? Why?

Review 4:12–13.

God's Word is alive because *God Himself is alive*. Jesus is the living Word made flesh, and the Spirit breathes life into the written Word, so it still speaks with power today. Scripture doesn't just sit on the page—it moves toward us. It reaches every part of who we are, exposing motives, desires, and the places we'd rather keep hidden. It's been said, "He's a surgeon, not a butcher: His Word cuts, but always to heal." And the same God who speaks through His Word also sees everything in us—nothing is off the table, nothing is unseen. That exposure isn't meant to shame us; it prepares us for grace and points us straight to Jesus, our great high priest.

★ 6. Where do you sense God's Word gently "cutting" in your life right now? How are you responding?

DAY 5

Hebrews 4:14–16

READ HEBREWS 4:14–16

Review 4:14.

In today's reading, the author pulled back the curtain on one of the biggest truths in the book of Hebrews: Jesus is our great high priest. Under the old covenant, the high priest could step into God's presence only once a year, but Jesus has passed through the heavens and is sitting at the Father's right hand. The writer called Him "Jesus, the Son of God"—a reminder that He's both fully human and fully divine. He knows our weaknesses, and He has the power to save.

That's why the author urges the Hebrews to "hold fast [their] confession." This isn't about confessing sin—it's about reminding themselves of what is true. Confession is acknowledging truth before God, while profession is declaring that truth to others. So when life got hard, the Hebrews were to cling tighter to what they already knew was true, then prayerfully declare the truth they believed *to* God: Jesus is exactly who He says He is, and He's the one who keeps us faithful to the end!

★ 1. What truth about Jesus and His character do you most need to remind yourself of as you hold fast to Him today?

2. Write a prayer using this type of confession. Thank God for who He is and what He has done for you.

Review 4:15.

The word *sympathize* literally means "to suffer with." Our great high priest isn't distant or detached. He sympathized with the Hebrews' weaknesses, and He sympathizes with our weaknesses too! Jesus knows what it feels like to be tired, tempted, misunderstood, and pulled in a thousand directions. He faced the full spectrum of temptation—physical, emotional, spiritual—yet He never sinned.

Temptation itself isn't sin; giving in to temptation is. Jesus felt the pull without crossing the line, which means His obedience is perfect and His sacrifice is enough. He's both the one who fully understands us and the one who can save us completely. That's why we can come to Him without fear. His sympathy draws us close, and His sinlessness keeps us secure.

3. Review the list below. Circle all the temptations and cross out all the sins.

Considering lying to avoid consequences
Stealing
Feeling envy
Speaking negatively of others
Hearing gossip and considering joining in
Feeling the pull toward pride
Lusting
Lying
Desiring to lash out in anger
Gossiping

★ 4. What keeps you from drawing near with confidence to the God who already knows you completely?

Review 4:16.

Because Jesus is our sympathetic and sinless high priest, we can *draw near* to the throne of God with confidence. And this throne—which is adjacent to fear and judgment for those who aren't in God's family—is the throne of *grace* for everyone who belongs to Jesus. For the believer, it's the place where God's favor flows freely, not because we're worthy, but because Christ intercedes for us. And when we come, we're promised two things: mercy and grace.

Mercy is God not giving us the punishment we deserve; grace is God giving us the help, strength, and favor we could never earn. (In short, mercy is when we don't get what we deserve, and grace is when we get what we don't deserve.) Both meet us right where we are, right when we need them. We never outgrow our need for this kind of help—and the good news is, we never exhaust His supply. He's where the joy is!

5. What stood out to you most in this week's study? Why?

6. What did you learn or relearn about God and His character this week?

DAY 6

Corresponding Psalm & Prayer

READ PSALM 95

1. What correlation do you see between Psalm 95 and this week's study?

2. What portions of this psalm stand out to you most?

3. Close by praying this prayer aloud:

Father,

You are my great God, my great King above all gods. In Your hand are the depths of the earth and the heights of the mountains. Jesus,

You are the great high priest who has passed through the heavens. Spirit, You speak through Your Word yesterday and today!

Lord, You are pure and holy. But the dirty dishes have piled up in my sink. Like the Israelites, I've sometimes hardened my heart. You've rescued me, but even still, there are times when I don't trust You. And like the Hebrews, I haven't always believed You. You've saved me, but even still, there are times when I don't rest in You. I'm sorry. You are the God of forgiveness—for the Israelites, for the Hebrews, and for me. Thank You.

I'd love to hear Your voice today, God. Help me not to harden my heart. Will You help me meditate on the truth? I want to hold fast my confession. I want to draw near to the throne of grace. Grant me a reverent confidence that all Your promises are true. I am a willing servant in Your house, deeply loved and humbly Yours.

You're better than Moses and all of the high priests of old. May my worship honor Your position. I surrender my life to You, Lord—every moment of my day, each decision I make, I yield my will and way to Your perfect will and way.

I love You too. Amen.

DAY 7

Rest, Catch Up, or Dig Deeper

WEEKLY CHALLENGE

On Day 3, we learned that belief leads to experiencing God's rest. The only way to God (and His rest) is through faith in Jesus. For this activity, think of one person in your life who needs to clearly hear the good news. Write their name at the top of a page in your journal. Underneath it, write out a brief, straightforward explanation of the gospel. Make a plan to share the gospel with that person. End by praying for courage, clarity, and an open door to share the truth that leads to real and lasting rest.

WEEK 3

Hebrews 5–6

Scripture to Memorize

Consider him who endured from sinners such hostility against himself, so that you may not grow weary or fainthearted.

Hebrews 12:3

DAILY BIBLE READING

Day 1: Hebrews 5:1–10

Day 2: Hebrews 5:11–14

Day 3: Hebrews 6:1–8

Day 4: Hebrews 6:9–12

Day 5: Hebrews 6:13–20

Day 6: Psalm 2

Day 7: Catch-Up Day

Corresponds to Day 355 of *The Bible Recap.*

WEEKLY CHALLENGE

See page 79 for more information.

DAY 1

Hebrews 5:1–10

READ HEBREWS 5:1–10

Keeping in mind that chapter and verse numbers were added to biblical texts long after they were written, we begin our study this week where we left off last week. Let's start with a quick review.

1. Complete the sentence below, summarizing 4:14–15. Use the word bank if needed.

Jesus, our ________ ________ ________, was tempted as we are, but is ________ ________.

high	sin	priest	without	great

Continuing in the discussion that proves Jesus is better, the author compared Jesus with the high priests who had gone before Him.

Review 5:1–4.

Being Israel's high priest wasn't a job someone could apply for. It was a by-appointment-only role, and the only one who could do the appointing was God Himself. God appointed Aaron as the first high priest of Israel and set apart his family, designating them as the priestly line.

2. Whose sins did the high priest offer sacrifices for?

__________ and __________

★ 3. How did that enable the high priest to "deal gently with the ignorant and wayward"?

The ultimate high priest, Jesus, was also appointed by God, and He also deals gently with the ignorant and wayward. But His gentleness in dealing with sinners isn't a result of His own sin (He has none). It's part of His perfection.

Review 5:5–6.

Quoting Psalm 2:7 and 110:4, the author introduced a new character: Melchizedek. We'll learn more about him next week, but for now, just note that he was a king and a priest whose story is recorded in Genesis 14.

Review 5:7–8.

Though He was without sin, Jesus lived a fully human life—one marked by prayers and supplications. Throughout His life, Jesus's prayers were both constant and sincere. He prayed alone in the dark of early morning (Mark 1:35). He prayed in front of a multitude of His disciples (Matthew 6:9–13). He prayed in agony as He waited for His arrest (Matthew 26:39). And He prayed with His final anguished breaths on the cross as He died a death only sinners deserve (Luke 23:46).

A recurring theme of Jesus's prayers was accepting His Father's will. Jesus chose obedience (John 10:17–18), and He lived it out so that His mission and purpose would be fulfilled. And from His example, we see that obedience is learned by living it—no matter what we endure through or because of it.

★ 4. In what ways are you learning obedience right now? Is that obedience costing you something? How does Jesus's example challenge or encourage you?

Review 5:9–10.

5. **Use a Greek lexicon to look up the definitions of the words from 5:9.**

ESV Translation	Greek Word	Meaning
being made perfect	*teleioō*	
the source	*aitios*	

Jesus lived a perfect life, carrying it through to completion. Dying as the ultimate unblemished sacrifice, He wrote the salvation story for all who obey Him.

DAY 2

Hebrews 5:11–14

READ HEBREWS 5:11–14

"There's so much more to tell you about our ultimate high priest," the writer essentially told the Hebrews. *"But it's really hard to teach people who aren't learning."*

The author's frustration isn't hard to find: He had to put the teaching about the High Priest on hold while he addressed a problem that seems to have been prevalent among the Hebrew Christians. It's a problem so big that we'll touch on it for the next three days.

Review 5:11.

1. The Hebrews had become "dull of hearing." What kind of problem is this? Circle your answer below. Use a Bible study tool if needed.

a physical disability

a heart problem

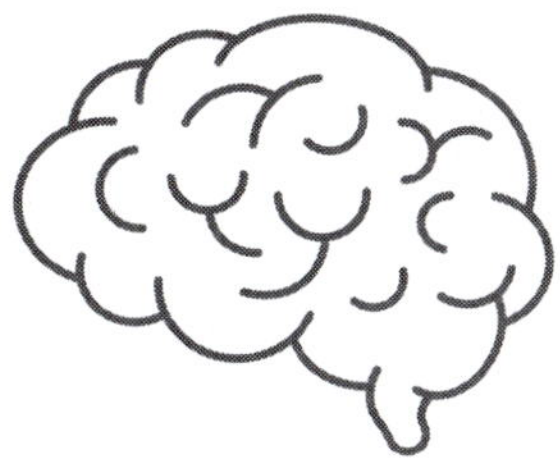

a limited capacity for learning

Review 5:12a.

By this point, the Hebrews should have been teachers, but instead they needed to be taught "the elementary truths of God's word all over again" (5:12 NIV). There's nothing wrong with needing to be taught. It's what the Hebrews needed to be *re*-taught that troubled the author: the basics.

This text highlights two important aspects of our lives as believers: We must *be* disciples and we must *make* disciples (Matthew 28:19–20). *Disciple* means "learner," and we must always be learning (Proverbs 18:15; 2 Peter 3:18). And we must also teach. For some of us, that means publicly teaching many. For others, that means personally teaching a few.

Review 5:12b–14.

2. Using the author's metaphor, match the phrases below.

Those who need milk are	mature, who have their powers of discernment trained by constant practice to distinguish good from evil
Those who live on solid food are	children, unskilled in the word of righteousness

For the Hebrews and for us today, the skill of discernment is developed through practice. That skill is a mark of spiritual maturity. So spiritual maturity doesn't happen automatically; it's not merely a matter of time.

God does the work of making believers mature—more like Himself (1 Corinthians 1:30; 1 Thessalonians 5:23). And His work calls for our active engagement.

★ 3. Do you actively engage in learning about God (being a disciple)? Mark your place on the scale. (If you need some encouragement, keep in mind that you're doing this study!)

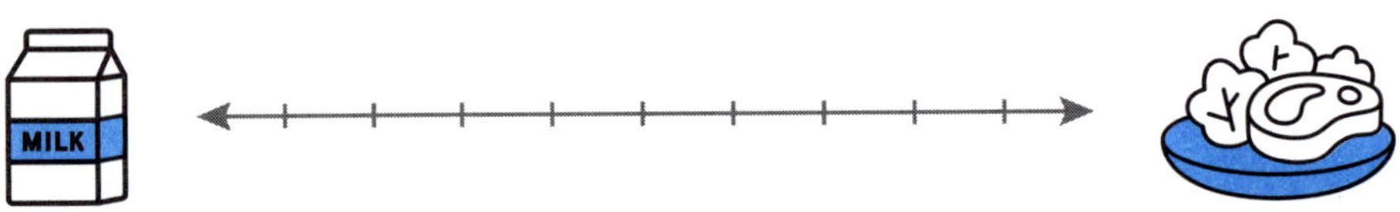

★ 4. Do you actively engage in teaching others about God (making disciples)? Mark your place on the scale.

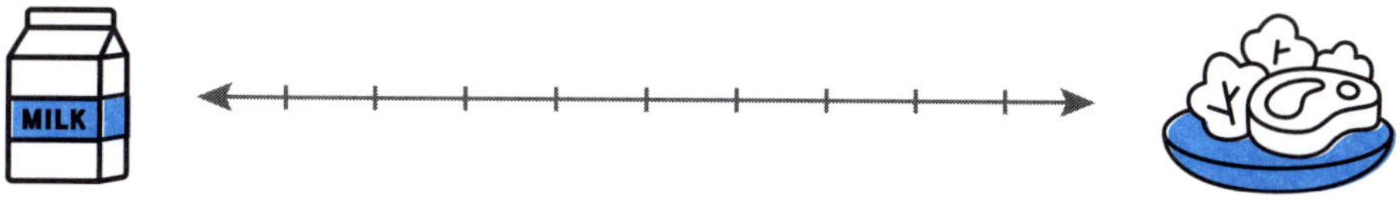

5. Write a prayer asking God to continue growing you in spiritual maturity. Surrender the places where you most need Him to move you from milk to solid food.

DAY 3

Hebrews 6:1–8

READ HEBREWS 6:1–8

Channeling his frustration into encouragement, the author urged the Hebrews to keep moving toward maturity. After all, they already knew the basics.

Review 6:1–2.

1. What was the elementary doctrine that the Hebrews already knew? Complete the blanks on the image below.

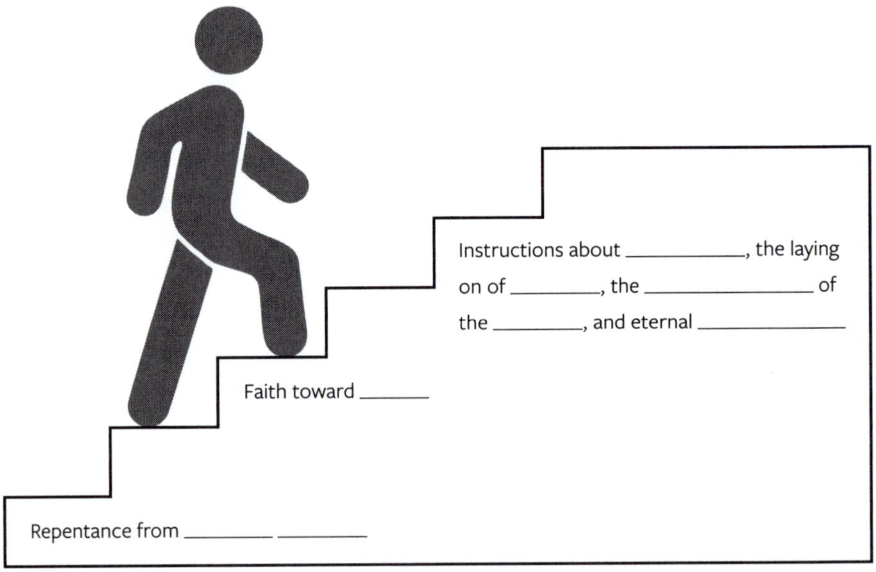

It's notable that all of these teachings about God would have felt familiar—and even comfortable—to the Hebrews. These were all principles of the Old

Testament law.[1] When these new believers were facing confusion, doubt, and even persecution, stepping back into what they already knew as Jews would've felt like the safest choice. But as the author already pointed out (and as he'll point out again), that foundation is good, but Jesus is better.

Review 6:3.

2. What would the Hebrews do if God permitted them? (Hint: Go back to 6:1 if needed. These three verses are part of a single connected thought.)

The remainder of today's passage has the potential to cause confusion, but like the Hebrews, we're called to keep moving toward maturity. So if God permits, let us leave the elementary doctrine and study hard things together.

Review 6:4–6.

First, the author gave a non-example; he described what moving toward maturity in Christ *doesn't* look like.

★ 3. Match each description with its likely meaning.

who have once been enlightened	have experienced a general blessing of Christian fellowship
who have tasted the heavenly gift	have read and/or heard God's Word and know about His coming kingdom
who have shared in the Holy Spirit	were taught about the Christian faith
who have tasted the goodness of the word of God and the powers of the age to come	have rejected the teachings they were exposed to and the community they experienced
who have then fallen away	have been in proximity to believers in whom the Holy Spirit works and dwells

This list may sound like it describes believers, but because Scripture should always be interpreted by Scripture, let's pause to notice what's *not* here. In Acts 16:30–31, the Philippian jailer asked Paul and Silas, "What must I do to be saved?" They responded, "Believe in the Lord Jesus, and you will be saved." And in Romans 10:9, Paul wrote, "If you confess with your mouth that Jesus is Lord and believe in your heart that God raised him from the dead, you will be saved." And even Jesus Himself, when asked what God requires, said in John 6:29, "This is the work of God, that you believe in him whom he has sent."

So why is 6:4–6 a *non-example* of believers moving toward maturity in Christ? Because the people it describes were never truly believers at all. They were exposed to God's goodness but weren't transformed by it. The list in 6:4–6 doesn't include any mention of their belief. They knew *about* Jesus but didn't believe in Him.

So after all of that, it would of course be impossible to be restored *again* as believers because *they weren't believers in the first place*. And after being in such proximity to Christ through His people, their rejection of Him was deliberate, prolonged, and so utterly vile that "by rejecting the Son of God, they themselves are nailing him to the cross once again and holding him up to public shame" (6:6 NLT).

But as for believers? They won't fall away, and they won't be cast out.

★ 4. Read John 6:37–40. How do Jesus's words reassure you?

Review 6:7–8.

Jesus Himself taught about belief using similar parables. The sower sows seeds on all kinds of soil. God sends rain on the just and on the unjust (Matthew 5:45), and the good soil produces grain, "some a hundredfold, some sixty, some thirty" (Matthew 13:8). But some soil bears thorns and thistles. And like all fields and vineyards in the ancient world that didn't produce a crop, it will be burned in the end.[2]

And as for the Hebrews? What kind of soil were they? Were they an example, or a non-example? Were they true believers, or just adjacent to some? Could they leave the elementary doctrine and go on to spiritual maturity?

We'll find out soon. But if your mind needs somewhere to rest after a hard day of study, take a sneak peek at 6:9, which is where we'll meet tomorrow.

DAY 4

Hebrews 6:9–12

READ HEBREWS 6:9–12

After hearing about people who spent time among Christ's followers but rejected Christ, we can imagine that the author's next words (in 6:9) felt like a deep exhale for the Hebrews.

Review 6:9.

1. How were the Hebrews different from the people in 6:4–6? What phrases from 6:9 point to that?

Though the Hebrews still needed to move into spiritual maturity, the writer was nonetheless confident that they were true believers. And how did he know? Their lives proved it.

Review 6:10.

2. How had the Hebrews shown their love for God?

Because of Christ, all believers are saints—the writer, the Hebrews, and us too. Because God first loved them (1 John 4:19), the Hebrews loved God and one another. And out of the overflow of their love for Him, they served their fellow saints—not to receive love, but to give love. Their service wasn't *for* love, it was *from* love. It demonstrated the sincerity of their belief in Christ and love for God.

★ 3. When you serve your fellow saints, is your service usually for love or from love? How can you tell the difference?

It seems that this body of believers in particular was marked by their service for one another, and the writer reassured them that he wasn't the only one taking note; God Himself saw them.

Review 6:11–12.

Knowing that service isn't easy, the writer encouraged the Hebrews to keep going: *"Don't get lazy. Keep loving God and serving each other!"*

There were countless believers who went before the Hebrews—and even more who have gone before us—whose lives were marked by faith and patience. Throughout their lives, they were confident that "all the promises of God find their Yes in him" (2 Corinthians 1:20).

And along with Christ, they were God's heirs (Romans 8:17). They didn't earn their inheritance; they believed in the one who *gave* it. And that belief was so deep in their bones that their everyday actions were marked by patience for the promise and faith in the Promise Maker.

When the writer encouraged the Hebrews to imitate those faithful believers, he certainly had a few biblical examples in mind; he wrote about many of them in this letter. But undoubtedly, the writer and the believers alike would have also thought about the many faithful examples in their communities—whose names and stories we don't know—people whose faith endured and whose patience persevered.

★ 4. Can you think of someone in your community whose faith has endured and whose patience has persevered? Write about them.

5. By following their example, how are you also following Jesus's example? (See Ephesians 5:1–2 and 1 Corinthians 11:1 for help if needed.)

DAY 5

Hebrews 6:13–20

READ HEBREWS 6:13–20

Sustained faith and patience have marked God's people for centuries. One of the earliest biblical examples we have is a man named Abraham. The author of Hebrews already mentioned him once in our study (see 2:16). It's hard to overstate the esteem the Hebrews would have held for Abraham. He was their founder—the patriarch of the Jewish faith. And even though Abraham lived long before Jesus's earthly ministry, his faith and patience are a model for Christ-followers today too.

Review 6:13–15.

Because Abraham's story spans Genesis 12–25, here's a quick summary: God made a covenant with Abraham. God promised that He'd give Abraham a land, that He would make him into a great nation, that his descendants would be as numerous as the stars in the sky, and that every family on earth would be blessed through his family.

But it didn't all happen right away. They faced opponents in the new land. Abraham was old and getting older. His wife Sarah was old and getting older. And twenty-five years after God promised them countless descendants, they still didn't have even a single child together.

1. What circumstances could have caused Abraham to lose faith and patience as he waited for God to fulfill His promise?

Like Abraham, the Hebrews had plenty of circumstances that could have caused them to lose faith and patience. As we've mentioned, they were facing intense persecution. We'll learn more about that soon; but for now, know that this meant their property, possessions, safety, and even lives were at stake.

★ 2. How would Abraham's story have encouraged the Hebrew believers?

Review 6:16–18.

When people want someone to know that their words are true, they swear an oath. In the first century, this meant swearing by deities, kings, or emperors.[1] People still do this today—being sworn in officially for testimony or duty, or even in conversation, swearing by their mother's life or by placing their hand on a Bible. They make their oaths by someone greater or more dependable than their word alone.

So how can God—the creator, sustainer, ruler, and Savior of the universe—make an oath? Only by Himself. There is nothing and no one else greater to swear by. He is our "strong encouragement to hold fast to the hope set before us."

Because Jesus had already been born, the Hebrews weren't waiting for the birth of the Messiah. But they *were* waiting for Him to return. Two thousand years later, as we write this study, so are we. His return is the glorious hope set before us.

This was strong encouragement for the Hebrews as they faced persecution. Because of this hope, they could endure. And still today, we have the same hope. When relationships fracture and the diagnosis is grim and bank accounts drain and loneliness weighs heavily, we have the same hope set before us. We have the same strong encouragement.

★ 3. In what areas of your life do you need to hold fast to the hope set before us? Write a prayer asking God for this strong encouragement to sustain you as you wait.

Review 6:19–20.

Circling back to the thought he began in 4:14, the writer reminded the Hebrews that Jesus is our great high priest. In the Old Testament, God dwelled in the Holy of Holies ("Most Holy Place" in the ESV)—the innermost space of the tabernacle (and later, the temple). This place was separated from the Holy Place by a tall, thick curtain made from animal skin called a veil. Only the high priest was allowed past the veil.

Our ultimate high priest Jesus went before us into the Holy of Holies, and He made a way for us. Because of Him, God's Spirit dwells in believers. We are anchored in the very hope that lives inside of us. That is strong encouragement indeed.

In 1834, Edward Mote, a pastor and hymn writer, put it this way:

> When darkness veils his lovely face,
> I rest on his unchanging grace;
> in every high and stormy gale,
> my anchor holds within the veil.[2]

Remember Abraham. Remember the Hebrews. Trust in God—in His promise and His oath. And hold fast, saints. No matter what we face while we wait, He's where the joy is!

4. What stood out to you most in this week's study? Why?

5. What did you learn or relearn about God and His character this week?

DAY 6

Corresponding Psalm & Prayer

READ PSALM 2

1. What correlation do you see between Psalm 2 and this week's study?

2. What portions of this psalm stand out to you most?

3. Close by praying this prayer aloud:

Father,

You are perfect, yet You deal gently with me. You are holy, yet You make me a saint. You own everything, yet You promise me a great inheritance. I am Yours, serving You with holy fear and rejoicing with grateful trembling.

But like the Israelites, I can be ignorant and wayward. And like the Hebrews, I can be dull of hearing. Both are heart problems, and I repent. Forgive me, Lord, and make my heart clean.

Lead me to leave the elementary doctrine and go on to maturity. I want to be a disciple, to keep learning about You all the days of my life. I want to make disciples, teaching others about You. Obedience is learned by living it, so help me, Lord. Provide the opportunities and the soft hearts and the true words. Lead me to obey.

You're better than Aaron and the whole priestly line. May my heart remember Your perfect sacrifice. I surrender my life to You, Lord—every moment of my day, each decision I make, I yield my will and way to Your perfect will and way.

I love You too. Amen.

DAY 7

Rest, Catch Up, or Dig Deeper

WEEKLY CHALLENGE

On Day 4, you wrote about the difference between serving for love and serving from love. One way you can serve from love is by starting with gratitude.

Write a list of at least ten specific things you can thank God for.

Is there anything on the list that you can give to another saint this week: a latte, a homemade dinner, a freshly cut lawn, childcare, or a game night?

Practice serving someone else in a tangible way—and out of the abundance of your gratitude for God's goodness to you.

WEEK 4

Hebrews 7

Scripture to Memorize

In your struggle against sin you have not yet resisted to the point of shedding your blood. And have you forgotten the exhortation that addresses you as sons?

Hebrews 12:4–5a

DAILY BIBLE READING

Day 1: Hebrews 7:1–3

Day 2: Hebrews 7:4–10

Day 3: Hebrews 7:11–14

Day 4: Hebrews 7:15–22

Day 5: Hebrews 7:23–28

Day 6: Psalm 110

Day 7: Catch-Up Day

Corresponds to Day 356 of *The Bible Recap*.

WEEKLY CHALLENGE

See page 99 for more information.

DAY 1

Hebrews 7:1–3

READ HEBREWS 7:1–3

The author has already mentioned the mysterious Melchizedek a few times. In last week's study, we learned his story comes from Genesis 14 and that he was both a king and a priest. Here in Hebrews 7, the author unpacked more about who Melchizedek was.

Melchizedek's significance influences this whole week of study, and it is key to understanding this chapter's main point. So let's dive into his story by going all the way back to Genesis.

Review 7:1–2a.

In Genesis 14:17–20, Abraham had just finished fighting a battle to save his nephew Lot from some enemy kings when Melchizedek entered the scene.

1. Read Genesis 14:17–20 and compare it with Hebrews 7:1–2a. Fill in the blanks below.

What were Melchizedek's two occupations? ________ ______ __________

Where was Melchizedek king? __________

Who did Melchizedek serve as priest? ______ _______ _______ ___ ____

______ _______ ____

What did Melchizedek bring? __________ ____ _______

Summarize Melchizedek's blessing. _____ _____ ____ _______ _____ _________

_______ __________ __________ _______ ___ __________. _____ __________

___ __________ ___ ____.

What did Abraham give Melchizedek? __ _______ ___ ______________

Melchizedek's first appearance was back in Genesis. Let's set the scene: Abraham had been called by God only a few chapters before this event, Israel didn't exist yet, and it would still be hundreds of years before they would conquer the promised land. Before Israel was even a nation, Scripture identified Melchizedek as a priest of the Most High God.

This means he was a priest serving Yahweh (the LORD) *before* God established the Levitical priestly system. We'll come back to this—it's an important theme that shows up again.

★ 2. **Use a Bible dictionary to look up *God Most High* or *Most High God*, and write what you find.**

Review 7:2b.

The author pointed out two important details about Melchizedek—one about his name and the other about where he ruled. The name *Melchizedek* means "king of righteousness." And Salem, which eventually became Jeru-*salem*, means "peace."

Melchizedek—a king and a priest—represented the noteworthy characteristics of righteousness and peace.

3. **Use a Greek lexicon to look up the words below.** Write their definitions.

Righteousness:

Peace:

Review 7:3.

In Genesis, Melchizedek quickly entered and exited the scene. He didn't show up again in any other Old Testament stories—that was his one shining moment (although Psalm 110 mentions him). In the Genesis account, there's no mention of his family or genealogy; we don't know where he was born or when he died.

Some scholars think this points to Melchizedek as a preincarnate Jesus —visiting Abraham two thousand years before Jesus was born in Bethlehem. Jesus has no beginning or end; likewise, this description of Melchizedek points toward an eternal figure—perhaps Jesus Himself.

Others see Melchizedek as a type of Christ; this is a way of saying Melchizedek foreshadows—or anticipates—Jesus. In this way, Melchizedek *resembled* Christ's eternal nature, but it's not a one-to-one comparison. Melchizedek's lack of genealogy doesn't mean he literally never died; but in the context of the story the absence of a genealogy helps to point forward to Jesus, the priest who truly lives forever.

★ 4. What similarities do you see between Melchizedek and Jesus? Use Bible study tools if you need help.

Let's review the key points of Melchizedek's story, because this purposeful history lesson sets the stage for the rest of this week's study.

5. Fill in the blanks below to review this section.

Melchizedek was a king and __________ with no genealogy. He represented the noteworthy characteristics of ____________ and peace. When Melchizedek and Abraham met, ____________ blessed Abraham, and Abraham gave ______________ a _________ of everything.

DAY 2

Hebrews 7:4–10

READ HEBREWS 7:4–10

Review 7:4.

Today's reading starts by building further on Melchizedek's interaction with Abraham, the highly revered patriarch of the Jewish faith. The author sums up his main point right away: Melchizedek was a great man!

Although the reason behind Abraham's tithe (giving a tenth) wasn't specifically mentioned, it's likely Abraham was expressing gratitude for Melchizedek's blessing. Abraham was also showing thanks to God through this gift, because Melchizedek was serving Yahweh as a priest. Abraham's tithe demonstrated that Melchizedek was greater than Abraham.

Review 7:5–6.

To better understand the author's argument, let's have another quick history lesson. Abraham was considered the father of the Jewish faith, and his descendants became known as the people of Israel, which consisted of twelve tribes.

1. On the next page, fill in the family tree with the name of the tribe mentioned in this section. Then look up Numbers 3:5–9 and write down what it says about this specific tribe. Note: Leave the top banner and the star blank—we'll fill those in later today and tomorrow.

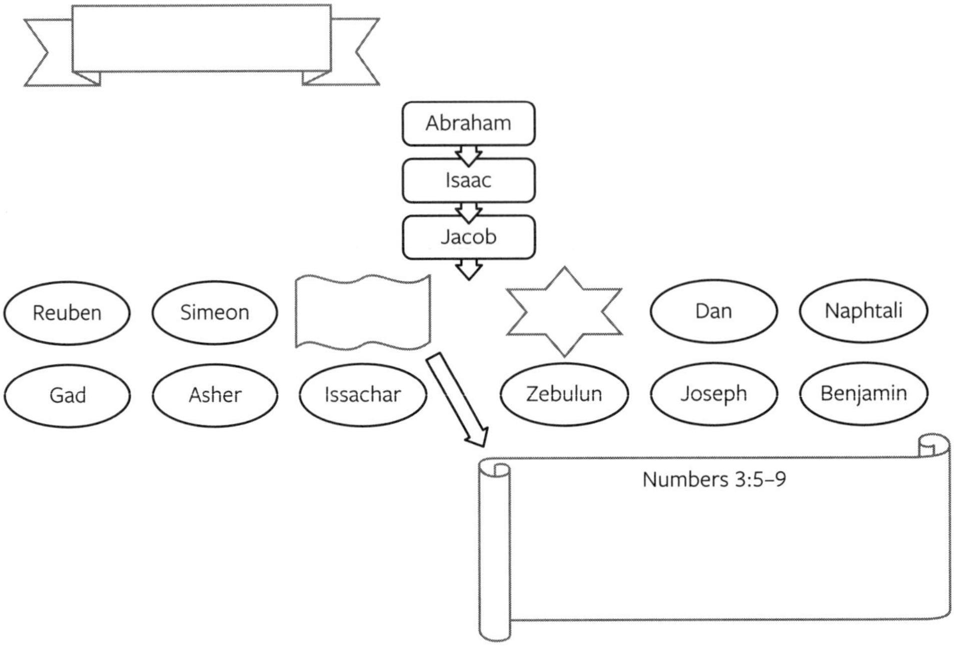

In Numbers 18:21, God made special provisions for the Levites because they were set apart in their work. The people of Israel financially supported the Levites through their tithes, because the Levites were ministering in the tabernacle. So even though all twelve tribes descended from Abraham, the Levites were the only tribe who received tithes.

So what does all this have to do with Melchizedek?

First, the author highlighted the fact that Melchizedek *wasn't* from the tribe of Levi, yet he still received tithes. It's important to note that Melchizedek's story predates the time when God made this special provision for the Levites. The tithes Melchizedek received weren't from the Israelites; God hadn't even established their nation yet. Instead, Melchizedek received his tithe from Abraham, who was the father of all the Israelites.

Second, Abraham had already received the promise from God that he would be a great nation and would be a blessing (Genesis 12:2–3). But instead of Abraham blessing Melchizedek, Melchizedek blessed Abraham!

★ 2. **Use a Bible dictionary to look up blessing.** Write the definition below. How does this inform your understanding of this story?

Review 7:7–8.

Based on the author's logic, Melchizedek should be considered greater than Abraham. (Remember, Abraham was the most highly respected patriarch of the Jewish faith.) The author wasn't making a disparaging remark by calling Abraham inferior. Instead, the author was highlighting this fact: However great his Jewish audience thought Abraham was, Melchizedek was obviously greater.

3. Write Melchizedek's name in the blank banner from today's first prompt.

Review 7:8–10.

★ 4. In your own words, explain the contrast the author presents in 7:8.

Wrapping up this section, the author made one final point: Levi—one of Jacob's twelve sons and the father of the priestly tribe of Israel—actually paid a tithe to Melchizedek through his grandfather Abraham. Although this might seem odd to us, the ancients held the view that the actions of their ancestors were connected to their descendants.[1] Therefore, when Abraham tithed to Melchizedek, Levi did as well.

5. In the family tree from today's first prompt, draw dollar signs connecting Levi to Melchizedek.

DAY 3

Hebrews 7:11–14

READ HEBREWS 7:11–14

Review 7:11–12.

In Exodus 28:1, God appointed Aaron and his sons to serve as His priests. God had established the Levites as the priestly line according to the law, and Aaron was a descendant of Levi.

1. On the family tree from yesterday's first prompt, write Aaron's name next to his tribe.

So if God established this priestly line Himself, why would the author of Hebrews be writing about another priestly line?

2. Fill in the blanks in the flowchart.

IF... ____________ was possible through the ____________ priesthood

THEN . . . there's no need for a priest to follow in ____________ order

SO . . . ____________ line (the Levitical priests) should continue

The key word for the author's argument is *perfection*, which we learned about in Weeks 1 and 3. We generally associate perfection with words like *flawless*, *ideal*, or *faultless*—but here, this word means "completion or fulfillment." Perfection is about bringing something to the full and complete state it was designed for, and this perfection was not possible through the Levitical priesthood (more on this in Hebrews 9–10).

★ 3. How does your understanding of the word *perfection* help you better grasp the author's argument? What questions do you still have about this word or topic?

Because God requires perfection, and perfection isn't possible through the Levitical priesthood, it's only logical to assume two things. First, there would need to be a change in the priesthood. God would provide a different way through an alternate priesthood—not the one established in the law. Second, because there was going to be a shift in the priesthood, there would have to be a change in the law as well.

Enter: a priest following in Melchizedek's order—one from a totally different tribe.

Review 7:13–14.

4. On the family tree on page 86, write *Judah* in the star and write *Jesus* next to His tribe.

The Levites served as priests based solely on their genealogy; there was no character assessment or job application for them to fill out. Yet Jesus, our great high priest, came not from the tribe of Levi but from the tribe of Judah—a non-priestly tribe that was given no instructions in the law about being priests. This was certainly unprecedented, but was it an accident or oversight? Of course not! Tomorrow we'll see that it was part of God's plan all along.

DAY 4

Hebrews 7:15–22

READ HEBREWS 7:15–22

Review 7:15–17.

In today's passage, the author builds on a few important things we learned about Melchizedek on Day 1 of this week's study.

1. Write a brief description of Melchizedek. (Hint: Look back at Day 1's first and fifth prompts for help).

In contrast to the Levitical priests who were appointed to their roles basely solely on their lineage, both Melchizedek and Jesus were appointed as priests by God Himself. Their priesthood was superior to that of the Levites because their fit for the role of priest was connected to their inner qualities and characteristics.

2. Circle the defining characteristic of Jesus's priesthood.

A. Jesus was a descendant of the tribe of Judah

B. His resurrection

C. Jesus was God's Son

D. The law pointed to Jesus

E. Psalm 110 said He would be a priest

"The power of an indestructible life" referred to Jesus's resurrection. Death couldn't defeat Jesus; therefore, He reigns forever as a king and serves eternally as a priest, full of both righteousness and peace. Christ belonged more to eternity than to any line of descent, and His immortality qualified Him to be a priest forever—just as God foretold in Psalm 110.

Review 7:18–19.

"A former commandment" refers to the laws concerning the Levitical priesthood. These had been set aside because Jesus was now the ultimate and superior high priest. Because of Christ, the Levitical priesthood was no longer necessary.

It might sound harsh for the author to refer to a commandment in the law as weak or useless, but keep his main message in mind: The law couldn't fulfill or complete the ultimate goal of salvation. Only Jesus could do that!

And because we have Jesus as our eternal high priest, we have a better hope. Because Jesus has made a way for us to draw near to God, we can approach God with full confidence and assurance. Jesus carries out the priestly work of standing before God on our behalf and making God known to us. He is the perfect mediator.

★ 3. What does it look like for you to "draw near to God"? Does what you've learned so far in your study impact your understanding of your relationship with Him? If so, how?

Review 7:20–21.

As if Jesus's indestructible life weren't enough to establish this new priesthood, God also swore an oath. The Levites were given no oath from God when they became priests. But as for Jesus? God promised that Jesus would be a priest forever—and He is! This will never change. The promise will never be broken, and God will never change His mind. God gave His word!

★ 4. How does God's faithfulness to His promises encourage you?

Review 7:22.

This verse is the summary and climax of the author's argument. Jesus provides the guarantee, fulfillment, and assurance of a better covenant, because He is a priest forever. God said so!

DAY 5

Hebrews 7:23–28

READ HEBREWS 7:23–28

This week's study wraps up with the author making two final points that highlight the supremacy of Jesus's high priesthood. First, His eternal nature and constant mediation benefit God's kids—that includes both the Hebrews and us! And second, His sinless perfection provided the perfect sacrifice by the perfect sacrificer.

Review 7:23–24.

1. Fill in the list on the next page by summarizing the author's arguments in 7:23–24. (Note: You'll fill in the rest of this table as we go.)

Review 7:25.

Save to the uttermost can also be translated *save completely*. At first, this phrase might seem like it's talking only about Jesus saving us from our sins. That's often what we think of when we hear the word *salvation*. And while that is where we recognize our starting point, the author's emphasis here is on the *completion* of salvation—the finish line!

Jesus saves to bring us to the end goal: our presence in His eternal kingdom. Jesus saves fully and completely. He will finish the work of salvation by ensuring His people reach their final destination: eternity with Him.

Jesus initiates the work of salvation. He sustains the work of salvation. And He fulfills the work of salvation. For us who look to Jesus as our great high priest, we can rest assured that our mediator constantly intercedes (prays) for us. His work is complete but His prayers continue (Romans 8:33–34; Isaiah 53:12).

Jesus as High Priest	Levitical High Priests
7:23–24—Jesus is eternal; therefore, He can be a priest forever. He will never be replaced as high priest. **7:25**—	**7:23–24**—
7:26–27—	**7:27**—
7:28—	**7:28**—The law appointed the high priests. Their weakness was their mortality and sinfulness.

Which priesthood is better? In your own words, explain why.

★ 2. How does the truth that Jesus is praying for you impact your relationship with Him?

3. In the table above, summarize the author's point from 7:25.

Review 7:26–28.

Besides being mortal, the high priests had to deal with their own sins before God. When they performed their sacrificial duties on behalf of the people of Israel, they also had to sacrifice on behalf of themselves (Leviticus 4:3–12).

But Jesus came and—on behalf of *all* humanity—sacrificed Himself, once for all time, so that whoever would believe in Him could draw near to God through Him. Jesus put an end not only to the need for sacrifices, but also to the need for special mediators between God and man. He serves as the ultimate, eternal, sinless high priest.

4. In the table above, summarize the author's points from 7:26–28, then answer the concluding question.

The Old Testament gave us glimpses of Jesus as our great high priest. Melchizedek's priesthood pointed forward to Jesus, and God's promise in Psalm 110 prophesied about Jesus. He is our high priest forever, God's own Son—the perfect mediator and the perfect sacrifice. He's where the joy is!

5. What stood out to you most in this week's study? Why?

★ 6. What did you learn or relearn about God and His character this week?

DAY 6

Corresponding Psalm & Prayer

READ PSALM 110

1. What correlation do you see between Psalm 110 and this week's study?

2. What portions of this psalm stand out to you most?

3. Close by praying this prayer aloud:

Father,

From Zion, You rule in the midst of Your enemies! You are God Most High. You have no beginning and no end. You are the Priest of Righteousness and the King of Peace.

But often, I've tried to put myself in Your place. I've wanted roles You haven't appointed me for. I've sought positions because of my heritage. I've boasted in my ability to keep the law. I'm sorry, God. Remind me who You are and who I am.

Jesus, remind me that You're praying for me, and that You give me everything I need for life and godliness. Form my words and direct my actions and guide my thoughts—I want all of them to look and sound like You. Spirit, help me draw near to You, today and every day.

Jesus, You're better than Abraham and Melchizedek. May my eyes focus on Your perfection. I surrender my life to You, Lord—every moment of my day, each decision I make, I yield my will and way to Your perfect will and way.

I love You too. Amen.

DAY 7

Rest, Catch Up, or Dig Deeper

WEEKLY CHALLENGE

On Day 4, we learned that we can draw near to God through Jesus's mediation as the better high priest. James 4:8 says, "Draw near to God, and he will draw near to you."

Take God up on His word this week and intentionally spend time drawing near to Him. Consider trying something new or different in your devotional time. Be creative and deliberate.

You could try corporate or personal prayer, corporate or personal singing, listening to a sermon, confession, spending time with Him in nature, Scripture memorization, Scripture meditation, or Scripture reading.

During your devotional time, be sure to thank Jesus that He made it possible for us to draw near to the Father.

WEEK 5

Hebrews 8

Scripture to Memorize

"My son, do not regard lightly the discipline of the Lord, nor be weary when reproved by him."

Hebrews 12:5b

DAILY BIBLE READING

Day 1: Hebrews 8:1–3
Day 2: Hebrews 8:4–7
Day 3: Hebrews 8:8–9
Day 4: Hebrews 8:10–12
Day 5: Hebrews 8:13
Day 6: Psalm 99
Day 7: Catch-Up Day

Corresponds to Day 356 of *The Bible Recap*.

WEEKLY CHALLENGE

See page 119 for more information.

DAY 1

Hebrews 8:1–3

READ HEBREWS 8:1–3

Review 8:1.

Hebrews is a beautifully cohesive book, the truth in one section often illuminating the truth in the one that follows it. And this verse summarizes everything we learned last week about Jesus as the great high priest.

1. Using Hebrews 7 as your guide, put a checkmark by the statements that are true of Jesus as the great high priest.

- ☐ He was a Levite.
- ☐ He is a priest in the order of Melchizedek.
- ☐ He offers His sacrifice(s) day after day, like the earthly priests.
- ☐ He sacrificed for our sins once for all time when He offered Himself.
- ☐ He has become the guarantor of a better covenant.

★ **2. Look back at 7:27. What in this verse indicates why Jesus is seated in 8:1?**

Jesus sits in the position of all authority in heaven, because His work at Calvary is complete. When He breathed His last breath on the cross, He said, "It is finished" (John 19:30). His is not an ongoing sacrifice; it is a *once-for-all-time, singular sacrifice* (Hebrews 10:12, 14). Because His sacrifice is complete, there's no longer any need for sacrifices to be made.

Priests in ancient Israel did not sit often; there was too much work to be done. But Jesus can sit because He has finished the work. There is no longer any work required for us to have communion with God and to be with Him forever. This verse points us to the good news of the gospel! Jesus has done all that the Father requires of us!

Review 8:2–3.

Throughout Scripture, we see God's heart is to dwell with His people. He wants to be with us. And He's always been very hands-on in making sure there's a way to do that.

3. Complete God's instructions to Moses in the wilderness in Exodus 25:8–9 (NIV).

> "Then have them make a sanctuary for me, and I will dwell among them.
>
> Make this tabernacle and all its furnishings _____ _____ _____ _____ _____
>
> _____ _____ _____."

This tabernacle, which can be defined as a "dwelling place," was also referred to as a tent or the Tent of Meeting. We'll get into more detail about the special pattern of this tent tomorrow, so stay tuned.

For now, we'll focus on the fact that 8:2 calls the place Jesus ministers the *true* tent.

4. According to 8:2, who set up the true tent?

The book of Hebrews was written to a Jewish Christian audience. To the Jews of this era, there was no place more sacred or holy than the temple in Jerusalem (which was the permanent version of the tabernacle they'd built in the wilderness).

This temple was the "tent" where the earthly priests ministered, sacrificed, and met with God on the people's behalf. But the author of Hebrews was telling this Jewish audience that, through Jesus, the Lord had set up a better tent for them, a superior and everlasting tent.

This week we'll discover why this true tent's existence was such an encouragement for the Jewish Christians then—and equally great news for us now.

What the author is establishing here is a change in covenants. We'll dig deeper into this as the week goes on.

★ 5. What was the gift and sacrifice your great high priest Jesus offered in 8:3? How does this illuminate your understanding of God's heart and His ways?

DAY 2

Hebrews 8:4–7

READ HEBREWS 8:4–7

The rest of our study this week will cover the differences between the old covenant and the new covenant. We'll be following along with the author as he compares these two covenants to illustrate the superiority of the new covenant. The comparison highlights the reasons why Jesus is better!

1. Correct the table by crossing out the descriptions that don't apply.

Old Covenant	New Covenant
Priests serve in the tabernacle, tent, or temple.	Priests serve in the tabernacle, tent, or temple.
The Great High Priest serves in the true tent.	The Great High Priest serves in the true tent.
Jesus is seated, because His sacrifice fulfilled the need for ongoing sacrifices.	Jesus is seated, because His sacrifice fulfilled the need for ongoing sacrifices.
Priests constantly make animal sacrifices to cover sins.	Priests constantly make animal sacrifices to cover sins.
Priests are of the Levite line.	Priests are of the Levite line.
The Great High Priest is of the order of Melchizedek.	The Great High Priest is of the order of Melchizedek.
Jesus is the priest.	Jesus is the priest.
Jesus is the sacrifice.	Jesus is the sacrifice.
Priests have to make sacrifices for the people *and* for their own sins.	Priests have to make sacrifices for the people *and* for their own sins.
Jesus is the sinless, spotless Lamb.	Jesus is the sinless, spotless Lamb.

In simplest terms, the word *covenant* means "promise"—like a binding agreement. The old covenant refers to the law God gave to Moses at Mount Sinai, which contained obligations for both God and His people so they could remain in relationship. The old covenant required animal sacrifices to atone for the sins that the people constantly committed. The old covenant was good, because it enabled the people to be in relationship with God.

But God had something even better planned. Enter: the new covenant.

Under the old covenant, being cleansed of sins required spotless animals, a temple, Levite priests, and the constant shedding of blood. Under the new covenant, blood was shed once for all time, eradicating the need to ever shed blood for the forgiveness of sins again (Matthew 26:28).

Review 8:4–5.

When Jesus came to earth, He was not born into the priestly Levite line. His birth fulfilled the Old Testament prophecies specifying that the Messiah would be born into the line of Judah (Genesis 49:10; Isaiah 11:1; Micah 5:2). But Jesus *is* of the line of the superior heavenly service—of which the earthly one is a copy.

When God gave Moses specific instructions about how to build the tabernacle under the old covenant (Exodus 25:40), those instructions were modeled after the superior version in heaven. That certainly adds an element of awe to the lengthy tabernacle-building instructions in Exodus (chapters 25–31, 35–40). Those were heavenly blueprints!

Review 8:6–7.

2. Why is the new covenant better?

3. Look up the Greek word for *mediate* (8:6). Write what you find.

The old covenant was good, but the people couldn't keep it—and in fact, no one but Jesus would ever be able to. By planning the new covenant, God had already prepared a better way dependent on only *His* perfect promise-keeping skills (Psalm 18:30). The new covenant had always been the plan the old covenant was pointing to (Revelation 13:8).

★ 4. How do you see the old covenant pointing to God's perfect plan in the new covenant?

★ 5. Do you recognize your inability to keep the laws and requirements of the old covenant? What parts of the system would've been most challenging for you (the laws themselves, the animal sacrifices, the required priestly mediator, etc.)?

DAY 3

Hebrews 8:8–9

READ HEBREWS 8:8–9

Throughout this letter, the author used the history of Israel to help his readers connect with the new covenant. Because he wrote primarily to Jewish Christians, they had a working knowledge of the Old Testament Scriptures. And they would have been able to personally testify to the superiority of the new covenant!

1. What Old Testament passage was the author of Hebrews quoting in 8:8–12? (Use a Bible study tool for help.)

Review 8:8.

Today we'll look at two Old Testament passages, Jeremiah 31:31–34 and 2 Kings 22–23, that are connected in a significant way. The authorship of the book of Jeremiah is attributed to the prophet Jeremiah, who lived from approximately 650 to 586 BC. Second Kings 22–23 describes the time of King Josiah of Judah, who lived around the same time—approximately 640–609 BC.

2. On the timeline below, write the names *Jeremiah* and *Josiah* over their corresponding dates. We'll come back to the final two dates later this week.

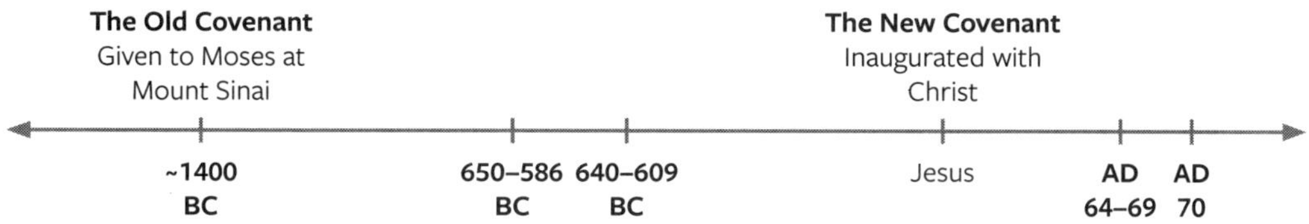

God gave the old covenant to Moses and the Hebrew people at Mount Sinai sometime around 1400 BC. But by the time King Josiah was on the throne, the people had forgotten God. They had even lost the scrolls, and many people had forgotten they existed!

According to 2 Kings 22–23, a priest named Hilkiah found the Book of the Covenant (the lost scrolls) in the temple. When King Josiah read it, he was grieved that the people had fallen away. He made a series of reforms—such as purging idolatry from the land—and he renewed the people's covenant with God (2 Kings 23:3).

The prophecy God inspired Jeremiah to write shortly after this event illustrates the great generosity, faithfulness, and mercy of God.

3. What did God say He would do in 8:8 (which quotes Jeremiah 31:31)?

"Behold, the days are coming" let the Hebrew audience know God had told them about this in advance.

In our modern understanding, we may see the word *new* and think *next* or even *another thing I don't need.* We see new products all the time that would only clutter our homes and lives. But when God says "new," He means "better."

There are two different words for *new* in Greek. *Neos* has to do with time. It can simply mean something was made recently, even if it's a copy of something that already exists. But *kainos*—which is the word used here—refers to both time and quality. It defines something that is truly new in its essence, and the implication is that it is *better*.

And this new (and better) covenant was not just for the people who lived in the days of Jeremiah. What began with the houses of Israel and Judah was intended for people from all the nations (Acts 1:8). It includes all God's kids!

Review 8:9.

Way back around 1400 BC, God took the Israelites by the hand, delivered them from slavery, led them through the Red Sea, guided them through the wilderness, gave them the old covenant, and then took them into the promised land. Miracle after miracle led them there. And it was in that deliverance and wilderness experience that the Lord taught His people to know Him.

But they let go of His hand. They broke their covenant with the God who had saved them. They complained that God had forgotten them.

But God was not content to let them go. Tomorrow we'll read more about His response to the people who doubted His love for them.

DAY 4

Hebrews 8:10–12

READ HEBREWS 8:10–12

As we open today, it's important to remember that the author of Hebrews was continuing to quote from Jeremiah 31. In our passage from yesterday's study, God explained what the new covenant would *not* be like. It would not be like the old one that was dependent upon the obedience of the people (Exodus 19:5a). The new covenant would be fulfilled by God's faithfulness alone (Ephesians 2:8–9).

Review 8:10–11.

1. Under the old covenant, where did Deuteronomy 6:8–9 say the commandments were to be written?

2. Under the new covenant, where did 8:10 say God would write the law?

Through the new covenant, God signaled a leveling up of individual intimacy —from the law's external regulation to the Spirit's internal transformation.

★ 3. You may find this offer of intimacy with God reassuring (Isaiah 43:1; Psalm 139). Or you may fear intimacy with God, for a variety of reasons. Explain your experience with this topic.

In 8:11, the author quotes the prophet Jeremiah, who seemed to joyfully and expectantly say, *"In the days of the new covenant, God's children won't have to tell one another to 'know the Lord,' because they already will! Everyone will be able to know Him, regardless of their standing by the measure of man."*

The prophet Jeremiah seemed so encouraged that the barriers would be removed between God and His kids. And the author of Hebrews wanted to remind his first-century audience that this incredible truth was available to them! The new covenant that had been promised was here, and they could know God!

Under the old covenant, there was a rigid standard of sacrifices, rituals, and rules to follow to walk in righteousness before God. Under the new covenant and in our new identity as God's kids, it's our transformed hearts that motivate us to live by His rules. We no longer have to sacrifice animals or follow rituals to draw near to His presence; because of Christ's work, the Holy Spirit Himself dwells in our hearts.

4. How does knowing God personally motivate you to live in a God-honoring way?

Review 8:12.

Have you ever vowed to "forgive and forget" when someone wronged you? We often have trouble keeping that promise. But God's promise-keeping abilities are not like ours. They're better (Numbers 23:19; 2 Timothy 2:13; Titus 1:2). And it's this profound truth that concludes the reference to Jeremiah 31:31–34.

Under the old covenant, the priests were required to make sacrifices constantly to cover the never-ending sins of the people. They were constantly working. But as we learned earlier in this week's study, Jesus's work as the great high priest canceled our sin debt once for all time.

God is merciful, but He is also just. Our sin debt had to be paid. And Jesus has already paid the price for our every sin (Colossians 2:14). God would be unjust to accept two payments. When God says He'll remember our sins no more, He means it.

5. Are there any sins or areas where it's hard for you to believe this? Write a prayer asking God to help you overcome your unbelief (Mark 9:24), and take God up on His invitation to intimacy with Him—the God who died to be with you.

DAY 5

Hebrews 8:13

READ HEBREWS 8:13

Christian persecution was common in the Roman Empire throughout the early church, but Nero, who ruled at the time of this letter, was particularly savage in his persecutions. He's known for lighting Christians on fire and using them as torches to light his garden parties.

Amid the rampant persecution during this time, the Jewish Christians who received this letter might have been tempted to revert to their old customs. In short, they might have thought, *Hey, we've got two covenants to choose from. Let's go back to the old one, because that one is less likely to get us killed.*

God made sure the author of Hebrews clarified why the new covenant was not an extra option, but, in fact, the better covenant and the replacement for the old covenant.

Review 8:13a.

The Greek word for *obsolete* in this verse is *palaioō*, "to be made old, to decay, to be worn out like wax."

1. Who speaks of a new covenant in this verse, and who does the "he" refer to?

The author of Hebrews was essentially telling the audience, *"It's not that God made a covenant that wore out like a watch and He needed to replace it."* The old covenant was never intended to last forever. It was always intended to be temporary—to make way for the new covenant that *would* last forever (Jeremiah 32:40; Ezekiel 16:60; Isaiah 55:3).

Review 8:13b.

In yesterday's study, we learned the new covenant ushered in access to greater individual intimacy with God. Under the old covenant, the temple (and previously the tabernacle) was where God dwelled with His people. The temple was central to their faith and practices.

2. What significant event in AD 70 involving the temple in Jerusalem lets you know 8:13b was prophetic?

3. Go back to your timeline in Day 3. Write *Hebrews written* and *temple destroyed* over the correct dates.

God knew when Hebrews was written that the temple in Jerusalem would soon be destroyed by the Roman army. This would have devastated the people, because the temple was where they met with God. But God's better plan was already in motion.

★ 4. Describe a time when trusting God's sovereignty helped you process discouragement or disappointment. (See Isaiah 46:10, Isaiah 55:8–9, and Malachi 3:1 if you need some encouragement right now.)

The new covenant was established on "better promises"—Jesus is called *Immanuel*, which means "God with us" (Isaiah 7:14; Matthew 1:23). Today, by His Spirit, God dwells in our hearts (Ephesians 3:17). And because we have been granted triumph over death, and because God's Spirit is eternal, no army can demolish His dwelling place. We will dwell with Him eternally (Revelation 21:3–4)!

The old covenant is obsolete—and this is good news. Jesus is the marker of the better covenant. And He's where the joy is!

★ 5. What stood out to you most in this week's study? Why?

6. What did you learn or relearn about God and His character this week?

DAY 6

Corresponding Psalm & Prayer

READ PSALM 99

1. What correlation do you see between Psalm 99 and this week's study?

2. What portions of this psalm stand out to you most?

3. Close by praying this prayer aloud:

Father,

You sit enthroned upon the cherubim, and the world quakes. You reign, and the people tremble. You are holy, and I worship You at Your holy mountain!

God, You gave us a covenant that You keep perfectly, but sometimes I doubt Your goodness. Jesus, Your work is complete, but I still strive as if I could earn my place in Your kingdom. Spirit, You dwell in Your people—including me—but there are times when I ignore Your promptings. I am doubtful, prideful, and sinful, and I repent.

Even as Your laws are written on my mind and heart, remind me that it's Your work—not mine—that made my salvation possible. Help me know and believe that Your sacrifice was enough. Help me to stop striving for my own salvation. Help me live as a person who is deeply loved by the Promise Maker and Promise Keeper.

You're better than the old covenant. May my desires rest in Your promise. I surrender my life to You, Lord—every moment of my day, each decision I make, I yield my will and way to Your perfect will and way.

I love You too. Amen.

DAY 7

Rest, Catch Up, or Dig Deeper

WEEKLY CHALLENGE

On Day 2, we learned the tabernacle God told Moses to construct was a copy and shadow of heavenly things—it was made according to the specific blueprint God showed Moses on the mountain.

Read Exodus 31:1–11 and search for any other occurrences of the skilled worker Bezalel in the book of Exodus.

Why do you think God enabled him and the other workers to do this work?

What aspect of your life can you ask Him to empower you for?

Actively ask Him for His help in those spaces as you move through your week.

WEEK 6

Hebrews 9

Scripture to Memorize

"For the Lord disciplines the one he loves, and chastises every son whom he receives." It is for discipline that you have to endure. God is treating you as sons.

Hebrews 12:6–7a

DAILY BIBLE READING

Day 1: Hebrews 9:1–5
Day 2: Hebrews 9:6–10
Day 3: Hebrews 9:11–14
Day 4: Hebrews 9:15–22
Day 5: Hebrews 9:23–28
Day 6: Psalm 24
Day 7: Catch-Up Day

Corresponds to Day 356 of *The Bible Recap.*

WEEKLY CHALLENGE

See page 140 for more information.

DAY 1

Hebrews 9:1–5

READ HEBREWS 9:1–5

1. Try to complete this pretest *from memory*. If you don't know an answer, simply put a question mark in the blank.

The Tabernacle

Who gave the building instructions?	
What was the design modeled after?	
What did it become?	
Who was the craftsman who helped build it?	
What three primary things did the Levitical priests do there?	
Bonus: List the seven parts of the tabernacle.	

Review 9:1.

The old covenant came with God-given, orderly instructions for worship and a specific place to carry them out: the tabernacle. Even though the Hebrews writer didn't use the word *tabernacle*, the original audience would have instantly known that's what he was talking about. (If they had to take today's pretest, they'd ace it—all their answers would be supported by Scripture, and they'd complete it in record time!) But our knowledge may not match the Hebrews' knowledge, so let's catch up!

OLD TESTAMENT TABERNACLE DIAGRAM

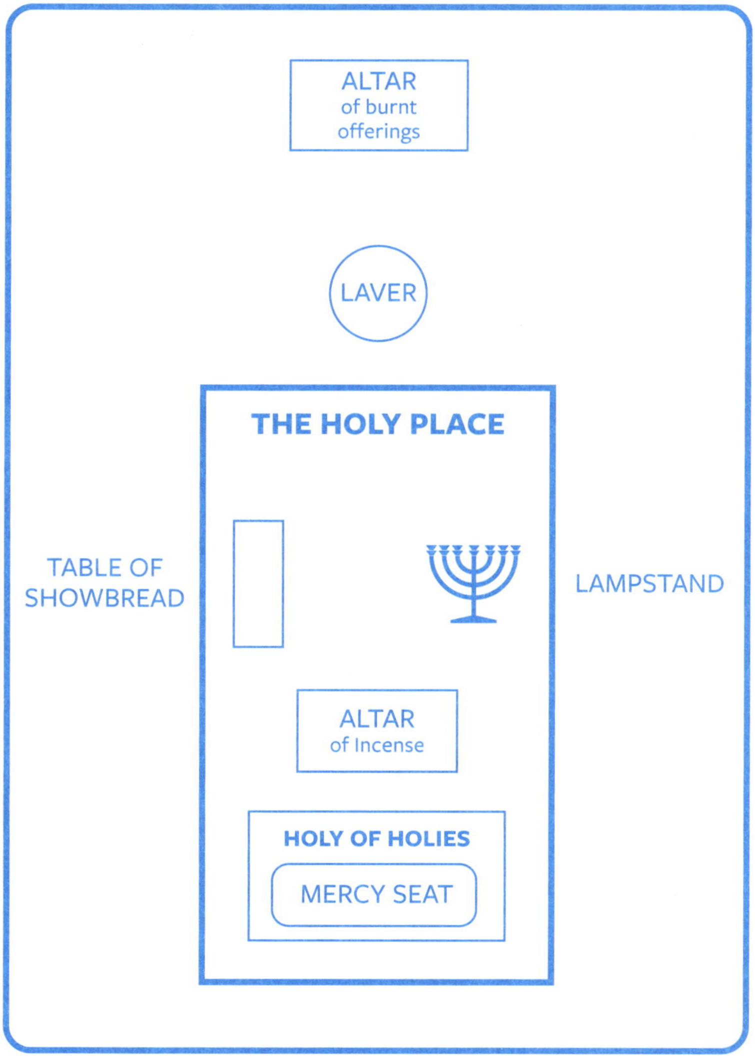

Note: The ark isn't pictured because it sat beneath the mercy seat; the mercy seat was its lid.

Review 9:2–5.

The tabernacle was the portable, God-designed dwelling place where God lived among His people and where Israel met with Him through priestly worship and sacrifice. The writer wasn't unpacking the specific details of each item in the tabernacle; he was highlighting how carefully everything was arranged. But remember, the Hebrews knew what each item was used for.

2. Complete the table below.

The Tabernacle

Item	Old Covenant Cross-Reference	Old Covenant Purpose
Altar of Burnt Offerings (*not mentioned in today's reading*)	Exodus 29:38–42	Priests made daily burnt offerings here so God would meet with His people. These were often blood sacrifices.
Laver/ Bronze Basin (*not mentioned in today's reading*)	Exodus 30:18–21	Priests *had to* wash their hands and feet here before entering or offering sacrifices "so that they may not die."
	Exodus 25:30; Leviticus 24:5–9	
	Exodus 27:20–21	Provided continual ________ in the Holy Place for priestly ministry.
	Exodus 30:7–10	Provided a perpetual, pleasing aroma before the Lord—an image of constant prayer, ____________, and purified worship rising to God
	Exodus 25:22	The high priest ________ ________ ________ and sprinkled _____ on this to atone for sin.

3. On the tabernacle blueprint above, circle each item referenced in today's passage.

In 9:3, the author moved past the first room to what lay behind the "second curtain"—the place most of Israel never saw—only the high priest could enter. A thick veil separated the Holy Place from the Most Holy Place. This was a vivid reminder that under the old covenant, direct access to

God was off-limits. Behind the curtain sat the Holy of Holies, where the very presence of God dwelled among His people.

4. On the tabernacle blueprint, draw a squiggly line above the title *Holy of Holies* to represent the curtain.

In 9:4, the author gave us a quick tour behind the veil, highlighting the golden altar of incense and the ark of the covenant. Even though Exodus says the altar of incense was outside the curtain (see blueprint), Hebrews ties it to the Most Holy Place. So if the altar of incense was physically outside the Holy of Holies, was the author of Hebrews getting this wrong?

The altar's function was to fill the Holy Place with the smoke of intercession on the Day of Atonement (more on that later). But just like the smell of a delicious meal baking in the kitchen might travel into the living room, the fragrant, worshipful aromas from the altar of incense probably wouldn't be stopped by a curtain. Most scholars assume the writer was pointing to the fragrant aroma drifting into the Holy of Holies.

Make no mistake: The writer wasn't just listing furniture; he was reminding his readers of the beauty and weight of old covenant worship. But even with all this gold and glory, it was still just a preview. All of these tabernacle details pointed forward to something better: the perfect work of Jesus, our greater high priest.

5. Look up these verses, and briefly summarize what each teaches about Jesus.

John 6:35—

John 8:12—

Ephesians 2:18—

Hebrews 7:25—

★ 6. Using what you learned in the prompt above, write each verse reference by its corresponding tabernacle element on the image on page 123. (Note: We've only included the pieces of furniture that are mentioned in today's text.)

★ 7. Would your prayer life change if you really believed you have the same access to God that only the high priest had once a year? If so, how?

DAY 2

Hebrews 9:6–10

READ HEBREWS 9:6–10

Review 9:6–7.

The author reminded the Hebrews that the old covenant revealed God's holiness and humanity's need for a mediator (someone who represents people before God). The priests entered the Holy Place every day. They maintained the oil and wicks for the lampstand, changed the bread, and burned the incense. Their daily work was constant, because under the old covenant, atonement was always needed. Access to God was still limited, and their ongoing ministry proved it.

1. In your own words, define *atonement*. If you need help, review Week 1, Day 5.

The priestly rhythms looked completely different on the Day of Atonement. This was the annual ceremony when the high priest entered the Most Holy Place with the blood of one goat and released a second "scapegoat" into the wilderness—symbolizing both the payment for sin and its removal from God's people. Regular priests could enter the first room often, but only the high priest could go farther, and he could do it only once a year and only with blood from the sacrifice.

2. Look back at the tabernacle blueprint from Day 1. Using a red pen, write "old covenant = once a year," in small print beside the Most Holy Place.

That once-a-year moment had strict requirements. The high priest entered the Most Holy Place with the goat's blood—first for his own sin, then for the people's, and even for sins committed in ignorance. Even unknown sin created distance from God, and the whole system made it clear: Israel needed a complete and permanent cleansing that these repeated sacrifices could never provide. This continual work and restricted access were meant to point forward to the perfect and once-for-all-time sacrifice of Jesus—the one who opens the way fully and finally.

3. Using large print, write "Jesus = The Better Sacrifice" at the top of the tabernacle blueprint.

Review 9:8.

The structure of the tabernacle wasn't arbitrary—it was divinely designed to *teach*. The Holy Spirit used its very architecture to show that under the old covenant, direct access to God was still blocked. The curtain separating the Holy Place from the Most Holy Place symbolized restricted fellowship with God. The first tabernacle "had standing." This meant the high priest was the only one who could pass behind the curtain. Access to God was not yet available.

★ **4. When did the veil tear? Briefly explain the meaning of the tearing. (If you need help, look back at Week 6, Day 1.)**

Review 9:9.

The whole old covenant system was like a giant object lesson. The tabernacle and its rituals pointed to something real, but they weren't the final solution for sin. They belonged to the former age before Jesus came, and they could never accomplish what our hearts truly needed.

The priests offered gifts and sacrifices repeatedly. And while those rituals could provide outward cleansing, they couldn't purify the worshiper once and for all. Their repetition proved their limits. But all of this was meant to create a longing for something better—and that "better" is Christ. He gives us access to God.

★ 5. Look back at yesterday's study. As you saw how every part of the tabernacle pointed to Jesus, what stood out most about who He is and what He's done for you?

Review 9:10.

This passage reminds us that the old covenant's rituals were always external and always temporary. Things like food laws (rules about what Israel could or couldn't eat), drink offerings (wine poured out before the Lord), and ceremonial washings (ritual baths that made someone "clean" for worship) could clean the body but never the heart. They were put in place only "until the time of reformation," a built-in hint that something better was coming.

That "better" arrived in Christ. When He came as the perfect high priest, He brought the true transformation the old system could only anticipate—a real, inward cleansing and direct access to God for all who believe.

DAY 3

Hebrews 9:11–14

READ HEBREWS 9:11–14

Review 9:11.

When Christ appeared, He fulfilled everything the old covenant merely anticipated. Unlike earthly priests serving in a temporary tabernacle, Jesus ministers in the true, heavenly sanctuary. His arrival turns symbols into substance—ushering in the long-awaited realities of full forgiveness, direct access to God, and lasting redemption. We've already learned that Christ is the better tabernacle, and today we see that He is the better sacrifice.

Review 9:12.

Jesus did what no priest under the old covenant could ever do: He entered the true heavenly sanctuary *once for all time*. Instead of repeatedly offering the sacrifices of goats and calves prescribed in Leviticus, He offered His own blood, giving Himself as the final and perfect sacrifice. This wasn't a temporary covering; it was a costly, personal, and complete act that secured eternal redemption.

★ 1. What repeated efforts or guilt cycles are you still trying to carry that Jesus's sacrifice has already settled?

Review 9:13–14.

2. What role did goats and bulls play on the Day of Atonement? Why were they necessary for Israel's cleansing? (Use a Bible study tool or read Leviticus 16 for help.)

There's a sharp contrast between the outward cleansing of the old covenant and the deep, inward cleansing Christ provides. Under the law, rituals involving the blood of goats and bulls and even the ashes of a heifer could make someone ceremonially clean.

The heifer (Numbers 19:1–10) was sacrificed outside the camp, and its ashes were mixed with water to create a purification solution. Anyone who became unclean—especially by touching a dead body—had to be sprinkled with that water so they could be made ceremonially clean again and rejoin the community in worship.

Christ's sacrifice, offered through the eternal Spirit and without blemish, reaches far deeper. His blood purifies the heart itself, freeing us from the guilt and "dead works" that could never give life. And this cleansing isn't merely removal—it's renewal. We're purified so that we can truly serve the living God with a whole, restored heart. He doesn't just take away the penalty of sin; He equips us for life!

★ 3. Where are you still try to deal with guilt through outward actions instead of trusting Christ's inward cleansing?

DAY 4

Hebrews 9:15–22

READ HEBREWS 9:15–22

1. Today's main idea comes from 9:22. Summarize it in your own words.

If you're squeamish, this passage might incline you to look away for a second—but don't miss what it's showing us. Blood represents both life and death. In the old covenant, the high priest always had to bring a sacrifice, because sin requires payment. We've seen this truth demonstrated since the beginning: From the very first sin in the garden of Eden, animals had to die to clothe Adam and Eve (Genesis 3:21).

Review 9:15.

The perfect high priest doesn't bring the sacrifice—He *is* the sacrifice. Jesus's death didn't just symbolize forgiveness; it accomplished it. And because He mediates this new covenant with His own blood, those who believe receive a secure, eternal inheritance guaranteed by Christ Himself.

Review 9:16–18.

A last will and testament takes effect when someone dies. This passage leans into that idea to help us understand the new covenant. The author used the dual meaning of the Greek word *diathēkē* (which can mean either "covenant" or "will") to show that in both cases, death is what puts the agreement into effect. In the same way, Christ's death wasn't just symbolic—it was essential. By dying, Jesus brought the old covenant to a close and launched the new one, guaranteeing that everyone who believes will receive the forever-life He promised.

2. How can the illustration of a will help us better understand what Jesus's death accomplished?

The first covenant began with blood—a clear sign that sin deserves death. Yet God allowed a substitute to stand in the sinner's place. Jesus's blood made forgiveness and fellowship possible, and His sacrifice pointed forward: Just as the old covenant started with animal sacrifice, the new covenant is established through the shed blood of Christ, the true and final substitute (see Exodus 24:5—the first time in Scripture when old covenant sacrifice occurred).

Review 9:19–20.

The author transported his readers back to Exodus 24, where Moses read God's commands to the people and then used blood to seal their relationship with Him. The additional details in Hebrews 9—goats, water, scarlet wool, hyssop—underline the same truth: Before sinful people could enter fellowship with a holy God, both the people and the written law had to be cleansed. When Moses said, "This is the blood of the covenant," he was pointing ahead to Jesus, whose own words at the Last Supper echoed that moment.

3. Review Matthew 26:26–28, Mark 14:22–24, and Luke 22:19–20. Which of these phrases weren't part of Jesus's words at the Last Supper?

A. "This is my body."
B. "I am the bread of life."
C. "This is my blood of the covenant."
D. "This cup is the new covenant in my blood."

★ 4. How does today's passage deepen your understanding of Jesus's words at the Last Supper?

Review 9:21–22.

The author continued with his recap of the Exodus story by noting that Moses also sprinkled the tabernacle and its vessels with blood—details not listed in Exodus but used here to make the point unmistakable. Under the old covenant, *everything* connected to worship had to be cleansed by blood. It was God's built-in reminder that sin is deadly, holiness matters, and forgiveness isn't cheap. Without the shedding of blood, there was no cleansing, no access, and no lasting fellowship with God.

★ 5. Jesus's payment for your sin was costly. Do you ever forget this truth and treat sin lightly? Explain.

DAY 5

Hebrews 9:23–28

READ HEBREWS 9:23–28

Review 9:23–26.

The tabernacle was only a small version of a preexisting heavenly reality—kind of like a scale model that serves as a 3-D representation of a real home, but in miniature form. It pointed beyond itself to the true, heavenly sanctuary where Christ now ministers. Through His ascension, Christ, the better sacrifice, entered the greater "tabernacle" of heaven. And He did it for our benefit (John 16:7).

1. Match each verse with its contents.

Hebrews 7:25	Christ is our advocate.
Romans 8:34	Jesus lives to make intercession for His kids.
1 John 2:1	Jesus is at the right hand of God, interceding for us.

2. What part of Christ's ongoing ministry (interceding, advocating, representing you) brings you the most comfort? Why?

Picture the priest making the same long walk into the Holy of Holies every year. If Christ's sacrifice were insufficient, He would have suffered repeatedly since the world began. Instead, picture Jesus stepping onto the stage of history one singular time, offering His own blood, and declaring the work finished (John 19:30). In that single, perfect sacrifice, He put away sin forever. His death was decisive, final, and utterly sufficient.

But His death was not the end.

Review 9:27–28.

Death is certain because sin is real. Principally, every person lives one life, dies one death, and then stands before God—no cycles of rebirth, no do-overs, no repeated lives. But that pattern sets the stage for Christ's own death: He died once for all time, but not for His own sin. His death was purposeful, voluntary, and redemptive (John 3:16). Jesus's *once-for-all-time* sacrifice was followed by a decisive resurrection. He triumphed over death! For those who believe, God's judgment over our lives isn't something to fear. Christ is the doorway of salvation for all who've placed their faith in Him (Romans 10:9–10; Ephesians 2:8–9).

★ 3. How does knowing Christ finished the work of salvation help you face the reality that your life will one day come to an end?

Just as Israel waited for the high priest to reappear from the Holy of Holies on the Day of Atonement, we now wait for Jesus. But unlike the high priest, who could potentially sin in the tabernacle and suffer death as a result (Exodus 28:33–35), Jesus's return carries a better kind of suspense:

anticipation. He's not returning to atone for sin *again*; that work is finished. Instead, He will appear a second time to bring the final, glorious salvation to those who eagerly wait for Him. He's worth waiting for! Truly, He's where the joy is!

★ 4. What comes to mind when you think about Jesus returning? Explain.

5. What stood out to you most in this week's study? Why?

6. What did you learn or relearn about God and His character this week?

DAY 6

Corresponding Psalm & Prayer

READ PSALM 24

1. What correlation do you see between Psalm 24 and this week's study?

2. What portions of this psalm stand out to you most?

3. Close by praying this prayer aloud:

Father,

You created the earth in all its fullness—the seas, the rivers, the land, and everything in them. Jesus, You are the once-for-all-time perfect sacrifice. Spirit, You dwelled among Your people and You dwell in Your people now. You were, You are, and You will be, and I praise You for it!

I want to ascend Your hill and stand in Your Holy Place, God, but my actions are halfhearted or hollow. And even when those actions appear righteous, I sometimes scheme or scoff on the inside. And after I've asked for Your forgiveness, I still try to deal with my guilt through my own dead works. I'm sorry. I want more than the removal of my sins, Lord—I want renewal.

Make my hands clean. Make my heart pure. You ripped the veil so that Your kids could be close to You, and that's where I want to be—every day of my life and for all eternity. Come quickly, Jesus.

You're better than the tabernacle and the temple. May my soul behold Your beauty. I surrender my life to You, Lord—every moment of my day, each decision I make, I yield my will and way to Your perfect will and way.

I love You too. Amen.

DAY 7

Rest, Catch Up, or Dig Deeper

WEEKLY CHALLENGE

On Day 1, we read about the tabernacle furniture. But our study didn't mention two pieces of tabernacle furniture: the bronze altar for burnt offerings and the bronze basin (laver). Let's dig deeper into these two pieces.

First, read the passages that describe them:

Bronze altar for burnt offerings—Exodus 27:1–8
Bronze basin (laver)—Exodus 30:17–21

Make notes on the tabernacle blueprint (page 123) indicating the following details:

- What the altar and basin were used for
- Who interacted with them
- Why they mattered for Israel's worship

After you have a better understanding of the original function of these furniture pieces, ask yourself: How does Christ fulfill what these objects symbolized? Use a study Bible or another Bible study tool to help you connect the dots.

Finally, write a short paragraph in your journal, answering this final question: What do the bronze altar for burnt offerings and the bronze basin help me understand about Christ's finished work?

WEEK 7

Hebrews 10

Scripture to Memorize

For what son is there whom his father does not discipline? If you are left without discipline, in which all have participated, then you are illegitimate children and not sons.

Hebrews 12:7b–8

DAILY BIBLE READING

Day 1: Hebrews 10:1–10

Day 2: Hebrews 10:11–18

Day 3: Hebrews 10:19–25

Day 4: Hebrews 10:26–31

Day 5: Hebrews 10:32–39

Day 6: Psalm 40

Day 7: Catch-Up Day

Corresponds to Day 356 of *The Bible Recap.*

WEEKLY CHALLENGE

See page 159 for more information.

DAY 1

Hebrews 10:1–10

READ HEBREWS 10:1–10

Our chapter begins with a transition word: *for*. So let's go back to the verses before it to ground ourselves in the writer's previous point.

★ 1. According to 9:22, what was needed under the law for the forgiveness of sins? According to 9:28, what did Jesus's sacrifice do?

Review 10:1.

A shadow can tell you a lot about the object or person it comes from—like shape, size, and movement. It can even tell you about the world around it, like the time of day or the season of the year. The shadow isn't the object itself, but it is shaped by and corresponds to the object.

As we've already learned, the law, including the sacrificial system, was given by God to His people. It was a temporary means to address an eternal problem: Sin separates all humanity from our holy God. And that sacrificial system, though temporary, pointed to the eternal solution: Jesus.

So the writer's point—to reinforce the theme we've seen more than once—is that the law was good, but Jesus is better.

Review 10:2–4.

2. How often did the priests in the Old Testament need to make sacrifices on behalf of the people? (Hint: You could read the whole book of Leviticus and keep a tally, or you can just look for the key word in Hebrews 10:1.)

3. What did all those sacrifices fail to do?

While the animal sacrifices symbolized the necessary payment for sin, they did not *accomplish* it. No animal's blood is worthy enough for that.

Review 10:5–7.

Quoting Psalm 40, the writer reminded the Hebrews that sacrifices and offerings themselves weren't the goal. God never intended His people to robotically adhere to a sacrificial system in order to be made holy. He wanted—and wants—His people to obey Him, to trust Him, and to have a righteous fear of Him (Hosea 6:6). He doesn't want rituals; He wants hearts.

Review 10:8–10.

As we've learned, the new covenant was ushered in by Jesus's birth, life, death, and resurrection. He came to do the Father's will, which He did perfectly. And in doing so, He established the covenant that makes us His.

★ 4. Describe the old covenant and the new covenant using words and phrases from 10:1–10.

Old Covenant	New Covenant
first	second
shadow	good things to come
continually	once

The blood of animals showed what was needed. Jesus's blood made the forgiveness of sins possible. The cross was not a down payment on a long-term installment plan. Jesus paid the cost in full, once for all time.

DAY 2

Hebrews 10:11–18

READ HEBREWS 10:11–18

If you're feeling a little bit of déjà vu after your first read-through of today's passage, then you're paying attention. Even though the writer had already spent a significant amount of time comparing the old sacrificial system with the new one, he had more to say. But rest assured: This may be repetitive, but it isn't redundant.

★ 1. Why do you think the writer so frequently reiterated ideas throughout this letter?

Review 10:11–13.

Under the old covenant, the priests made *continual* sacrifices. Their work was never finished. But as we learned in our study of 1:3 and 8:1, after Jesus sacrificed Himself once for all time, He sat down.

The significance of this seemingly simple act can't be overstated. In fact, Jesus Himself pointed to it throughout His ministry.

★ 2. Read the passages below, looking for Jesus's words and actions related to sitting down.

Passage	What did Jesus say?	What did Jesus do immediately after He spoke?	What does it mean?
Luke 4:16–20			
Matthew 22:41–45		Declared seven woes to the scribes and Pharisees.	That Jesus is the Messiah. He's not just David's "son" (descen-dant), but David's Lord.
Mark 14:53–65		He submitted Himself to the Father's will, giving Himself as our sacrifice.	

This truth of Jesus's work being finished comforts us today, but it was infuriating to the high priest in Mark 14. In fact, he tore his clothes and accused Jesus of blasphemy. Even though most of the religious leaders didn't understand that the entire Old Testament pointed forward to Jesus,

He had been telling them that all along. His work was perfect. His sacrifice was complete. The need for any further sacrifice would be gone.

Review 10:14.

In one verse, we see three distinct markers of every believer's journey in Christ: justification, sanctification, and glorification. *Justification* is the moment in which God declares a believer righteous because of Jesus's perfect sacrifice. *Sanctification* is the lifelong process of God making us more like Himself. *Glorification* is the completion of that process. It's the fulfillment of God's redemptive plan. It's when believers will be with God, sharing in His glory, forever.

3. Match each phrase from 10:14 NLT with the part of the believer's life that it describes.

Justification	he forever made perfect
Sanctification	by that one offering
Glorification	are being made holy

Review 10:15–18.

Like the writer did in 8:8, he again quoted from Jeremiah 31. God wants His people to remember His good law, putting it on their hearts and writing it on their minds. But He doesn't stop there.

4. Fill in the blanks in 10:17, quoted from Jeremiah 31.

"Then he ______, 'I will remember their ______ and their ______ deeds ______ ______.'"

The law was good. Jesus is better. Praise Him for His finished work!

DAY 3

Hebrews 10:19–25

READ HEBREWS 10:19–25

1. Use 10:19–25 to complete the chart below.

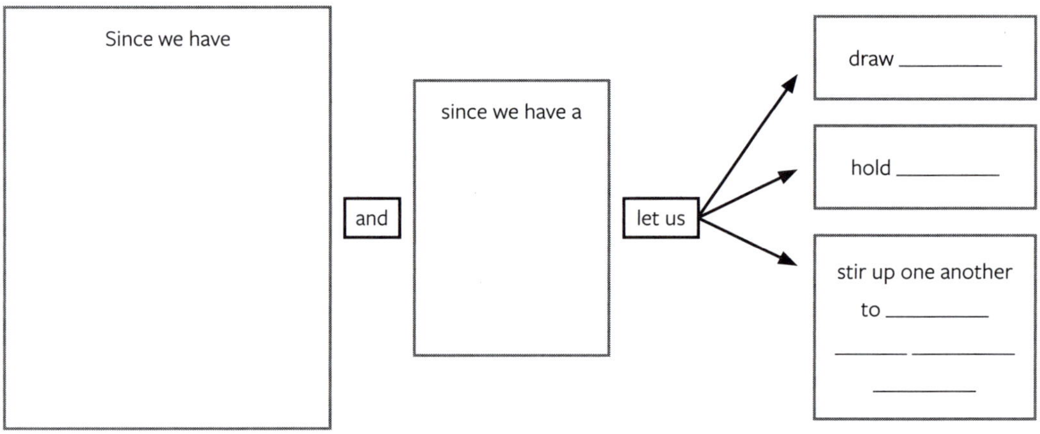

Review 10:19–21.

The author knew that the Hebrews could draw near, hold fast, and stir up one another to love and good works. And he also knew that the only reason they could do all of this was because of Jesus's finished work as our great high priest. By this point in the letter, he'd explained it many times.

And as they'd been encouraged to do in 5:12–6:3, they could practice moving forward and maturing in their faith by teaching it. And so can we!

2. In your own words, explain what it means that Jesus is our great high priest.

Because of our great high priest, believers are empowered in their daily lives to do certain things. The writer listed a few examples.

Review 10:22.

To draw near to our holy God, we must be clean. Jesus did that work on our behalf, so with full assurance in our Savior, we can go right into God's presence. Though our sins were like scarlet, Jesus made them white as snow.

Review 10:23.

Charles Spurgeon said, "That exhortation, 'Let us hold fast,' might well be written on the cover of every Christian's Bible. . . . We need all to be exhorted to be rooted and grounded, confirmed and established, in the truth."[1]

★ 3. What are some practical ways you can hold fast?

Review 10:24–25.

Some of the Hebrews had stopped meeting together with their brothers and sisters in Christ. Even though they faced the very real threat of persecution, the author reminded them that being together is vital. A beautiful aspect of the Christian life is that it's not meant to be lived alone.

And that doesn't just mean that we gather on Sunday mornings to be taught by our pastors. We need our brothers and sisters constantly. We need the daily, peer-to-peer "one another-ing" that's mentioned many times throughout the New Testament: to serve one another (1 Peter 4:10), love one another (John 13:34), encourage one another (1 Thessalonians 5:11), forgive one another (Colossians 3:13), and even sing to one another (Ephesians 5:19). And until the day of Christ's return, we need to keep doing this—stirring up one another to love and good works.

★ 4. What are some ways your brothers and sisters in Christ have stirred you up to love and good works?

DAY 4

Hebrews 10:26–31

READ HEBREWS 10:26–31

The writer moved on from stirring up one another to love and good works, taking what may seem like a hard left turn. But his train of thought isn't too hard to follow. In 10:25, he reminded the Hebrews that "the Day" was drawing near. For believers, that will be the glorious time when our Savior returns and our faith is made sight. But for everyone else?

1. Read Amos 5:18–20. What will the Day be like for those who do not believe in Christ Jesus?

Review 10:26–27.

Using the same lens through which we studied 6:4–8, someone who has "received the knowledge of the truth" has heard the good news about Jesus but hasn't believed in Him. And for that person, when Christ returns, there isn't another chance. It'll be too late.

The Hebrews were familiar with the Old Testament's many associations of God's judgment with fire. In Numbers 26:10, two hundred and fifty men who had rebelled against Moses and Aaron were devoured by fire. In Zephaniah 1:18, God's righteous jealousy is compared to fire. And in Isaiah 26:11, God's enemies are prophesied to be consumed by fire. The writer of Hebrews echoed that warning.

Review 10:28–29.

2. Read Leviticus 24:13–16. Under the law, what was the penalty for blasphemy?

The writer again described unbelieving people who were in proximity to believers. While the believers around them were being sanctified by God, these people had "treated the blood of the covenant, which made us holy, as if it were common and unholy" (10:29 NLT).

3. After having every opportunity to believe in Jesus but deciding to reject Him, what were these people guilty of? Fill in the blanks associated with 10:29.

Trampling _______ ____ ____ __ _____

Profaning ___ _______ ____ ____ ________

Outraging ___ ________ __ _____

4. How did the writer of Hebrews describe the punishment for these crimes?

While it might be a bit easier to stomach the reality of this punishment for abusers, enslavers, and murderers, the whole truth is that this is the just punishment for everyone who rejects Christ. And an even more sobering reminder is that this is the punishment we all deserve. As the saying goes, "There, but for the grace of God, go I." Literally. It is only because of our great high priest that those who believe in Him are not only spared from fire, but destined for glory.

Review 10:30–31.

The Day is drawing near. But before it comes, you have today. Pray, share, warn, encourage, teach, admonish, preach, pray again. May no one face the fearful thing until we've done all we can do.

★ 5. Write a prayer for someone you know who has rejected Christ.

★ 6. Write a prayer asking God to give you courage to share the gospel with them as many times as it takes.

DAY 5

Hebrews 10:32–39

READ HEBREWS 10:32–39

Reassuring the Hebrews that the day of the Lord would be joyful for them, the writer reminded them of the evidence of true faith in their lives.

Review 10:32–34.

1. What happened to the Hebrews after they became followers of Christ?

In the first-century Roman Empire, believers faced persecution not only from Jewish religious leaders, but also from the government. Legal authorities often took possession of the property of accused criminals. And it wasn't uncommon for the homes of the imprisoned to be looted.[1]

What's more, prisons in the first century were cruel. Conditions were barbaric, and captives weren't given any supplies—not even food.[2] So if no one brought them something to eat, they starved.

2. What did the Hebrew believers do for those in prison?

The Hebrews' lives hadn't been easy since they broke with Jewish tradition and decided to follow Christ. But they knew that what they gained in Him was worth more than what they'd ever lose by following Him. The author basically reminded them, "*They persecuted you and the people you love. They raided your homes and stole your belongings. But you knew your best possession was much more valuable. And it will last forever.*"

3. What was the Hebrews' better and abiding possession?

Review 10:35–36.

Reminding them again of their confidence in Christ and their promised reward, the author encouraged them once more that they needed endurance.

★ 4. **Use a Greek lexicon to look up *endurance* (10:36).** What do you notice?

Review 10:37–39.

Quoting again from the Old Testament, the writer turned to Habakkuk. In the book of Habakkuk, the people of Judah learned that God must punish all sin, and that God wants His people to live by faith. Both of these lessons given to Judah were also important for the Hebrews. And they're important for us today, as well.

★ 5. How would the exhortation to live by faith have encouraged the Hebrews? How does it encourage you?

"Shrinking back" is a posture of uncertainty, timidity, and fear (not the good kind). But "God gave us a spirit not of fear but of power and love and self-control" (2 Timothy 1:7). Regardless of the persecution the Hebrews faced, and regardless of the hardships you may face, living by faith requires a confident endurance—one that knows His promises are true and His reward is eternal.

Don't shrink back. Endure. Hold fast. He's where the joy is!

6. What stood out to you most in this week's study? Why?

7. What did you learn or relearn about God and His character this week?

DAY 6

Corresponding Psalm & Prayer

READ PSALM 40

1. What correlation do you see between Psalm 40 and this week's study?

2. What portions of this psalm stand out to you most?

3. Close by praying this prayer aloud:

Father,

Your steadfast love and faithfulness preserve me. You have multiplied Your wondrous deeds and Your thoughts toward me. Your promises are true and Your reward is eternal.

Like You did for David, You drew me up from the pit of destruction, out of the miry bog, and set my feet upon a rock. But I keep trying to go back to the bog, Lord. With my legalism, I weigh myself down trying to earn my own righteousness. With my licentiousness, I get myself stuck, insisting my freedom won't lead to sin. Both land me in the bog, and I repent. Thank You for remembering my sins and lawless deeds no more.

Will You put a new song in my mouth—a song of constant praise? The Day is drawing near, so teach me how to share Your good news with boldness and humility. May those who hear it put their trust in You.

You're better than the law. May my words proclaim Your gospel. I surrender my life to You, Lord—every moment of my day, each decision I make, I yield my will and way to Your perfect will and way.

I love You too. Amen.

DAY 7

Rest, Catch Up, or Dig Deeper

WEEKLY CHALLENGE

On Day 4, you wrote a prayer for someone you know who has rejected Christ. You also wrote a prayer asking God for courage to share the gospel with them.

This week, using whatever opportunities and methods the Lord brings to your mind, share the good news with that person.

WEEK 8

Hebrews 11

Scripture to Memorize

Besides this, we have had earthly fathers who disciplined us and we respected them. Shall we not much more be subject to the Father of spirits and live?

Hebrews 12:9

DAILY BIBLE READING

Day 1: Hebrews 11:1–7

Day 2: Hebrews 11:8–16

Day 3: Hebrews 11:17–22

Day 4: Hebrews 11:23–31

Day 5: Hebrews 11:32–40

Day 6: Psalm 18

Day 7: Catch-Up Day

Corresponds to Day 357 of *The Bible Recap.*

WEEKLY CHALLENGE

See page 181 for more information.

DAY 1

Hebrews 11:1–7

READ HEBREWS 11:1–7

This chapter is sometimes called the Faith Hall of Fame or the Hall of Faith.

Review 11:1–2.

1. How is faith defined? Circle all that apply.

   A. A feeling
   B. The assurance of things hoped for
   C. The evidence of things not seen
   D. An emotion

Faith is not a feeling that defies logic. Faith is the conviction of things that are true, but sometimes invisible to the human eye. Here on earth, we testify in faith to the truth of God's Word about what awaits us in eternity. But someday, we'll be experiencing it all, and faith will no longer be required (1 Corinthians 13:12; 1 John 3:2).

Faith is the evidence of what's to come—and evidence of what's true of God now.

Our faith is not vague—it's not a feeling or a vibe. Faith is always aware of its object. The Christian faith is a faith *in Christ*. He's who our faith points to, rests on, and is rooted in (Colossians 2:7).

Faith is also active. It produces results. Faith is not a matter of personality. James 2:18 says, "Someone will say, 'You have faith and I have works.' Show me your faith apart from your works, and I will show you my faith *by* my works" (emphasis added).

2. According to James 2:17, what is faith without action?

When the author of Hebrews told his audience what the ancients were commended for, he mentioned their *faith*, not their works. But James 2:17 is not in conflict with the message of Hebrews 11. Instead, these two passages work together to remind us that faith *produces* works. It turns unseen things into seen things—as our actions begin to reflect the internal transformation that has occurred in us. When we walk in faith, our lives testify to the world!

This week, we'll journey through forty verses—and these are perhaps Scripture's most action-packed summary of how God plants good works in people's hearts. And then, of course, *He does the doing* to bring them to pass.

Review 11:3–7.

Remember that this book was written to a Jewish Christian audience. They knew the Old Testament stories like the backs of their hands. Many early church fathers believed the world was made out of preexisting materials.[1] But the Hebrews author reminded his audience that they believed God created the world out of *nothing*—making what is seen out of what is unseen (Genesis 1–2).

3. Theologians use a Latin term to succinctly refer to this "creation out of nothing." Do a web search or use a Bible dictionary to look up the term, then fill in the blanks:

Creation out of nothing = *Creatio* ___ - _______

The Hebrews audience also believed that God created Adam and Eve; and from Adam and Eve came the first offspring, Cain and Abel (Genesis 4). And though Abel was murdered, his testimony of faithfulness to God was still ringing out thousands of years later.

The Hebrews author highlights here what may prove to be the biggest challenge for us as we engage with this chapter: pain and death.

Sometimes faith results in *overcoming* earthly circumstances. For instance, Enoch never died (Genesis 5:24). And his great-grandson Noah survived a flood because he obediently built an ark (Genesis 6–9).

Other times, faith results in persevering *despite* your earthly circumstances. The defiant testimony of these saints, amid suffering and even death, points others to the "better-ness" of Jesus.

★ 4. Explain a time when you witnessed or experienced a defiant testimony of faith amid suffering.

★ 5. What aspect of Hebrews 11:6 is most challenging or encouraging to you?

DAY 2

Hebrews 11:8–16

READ HEBREWS 11:8–16

The guiding principle we'll employ in today's study is "This is not our home." The world as we know it is not our ultimate destination. If you're in Christ, an eternal inheritance awaits you that cannot be shaken, taken away, marred, or stolen—not by anyone or anything. Through Abraham, we see God writing a story of His promise-keeping nature both during our earthly lives *and* in eternity.

Review 11:8–10.

1. Using 11:8–10, fill in the blanks below.

It's easy to look at earthly prosperity and assume it corresponds to God's approval of the prosperous person. But in Scripture, we see the saints experiencing a wide range of worldly wealth—from the fortunes of Solomon and Lydia to the poverty of the widow and the lowly estate of Joseph and Mary (1 Kings 10:14–27; Acts 16:14; Mark 12:41–44; Luke 2:24).

2. In 11:9, we're reminded of how God's people first entered the land of promise. What did they live in when they got there?

The tents—and the land of promise itself—were designed to be temporary. In Week 5, we learned that the tabernacle was a copy and shadow of the heavenly one (8:5). Here in 11:10, we find another hint about the eternity that awaits us: We've got a heavenly city that God Himself designed! And Abraham had his gaze set on eternity; it's what enabled him not only to endure, but to participate in God's fulfillment of His very good promises right here on earth.

Review 11:11–12.

The mention of Sarah in this passage highlights a trend we'll see throughout the chapter: *The people God uses aren't perfect.* What a relief.

Moments of weariness, discouragement, and disillusionment don't disqualify us from a life of faith. When God assured Sarah that she—after twenty-five years of waiting—would finally have a child, she laughed in disbelief (Genesis 18:9–15). But she had a son named Isaac, which means "laughter" (Genesis 21:6). Those nine months served to strengthen her faith in the God who fulfills His promises!

3. According to 11:12, what was the fruit of Sarah and Abraham's painful waiting season?

Abraham absolutely saw fulfillment of God's promises in his life on earth, even though he didn't see the *complete* fulfillment. Not only did he live to see the birth of his son Isaac, but he (almost certainly) got to meet his grandsons, Jacob and Esau, who were born when he was roughly 160 years old. Over the course of his long life, Abraham witnessed the early evidence of God's promises coming to fruition.

Review 11:13–16.

4. Which four people is 11:13 referring to? Look back at 11:8–12 for help and fill in their names below.

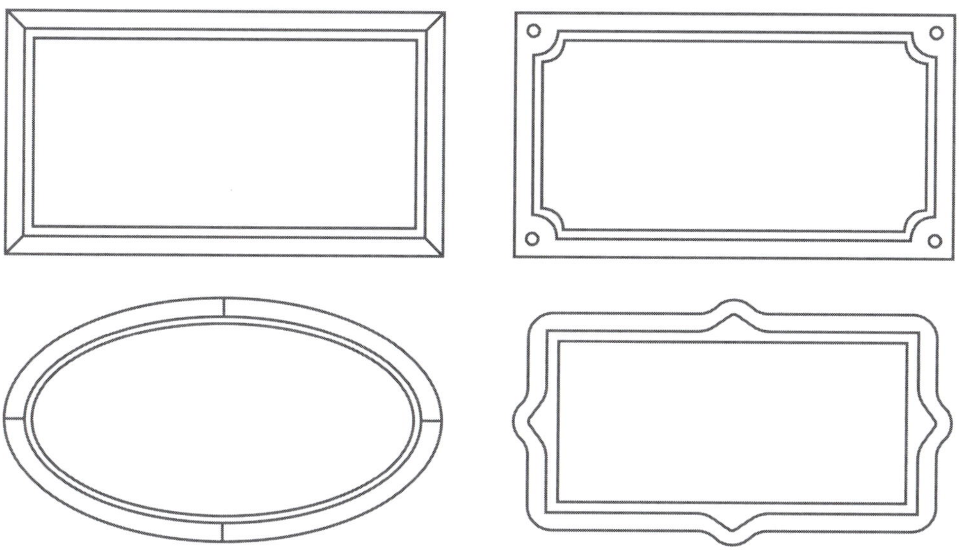

These saints saw God's fulfillment of His promises falling like a shadow on their path—it loomed in the distance. And while they walked that path as both literal and figurative nomads, they kept moving forward, eyes on the horizon.

Abraham was indeed seeking a homeland, but specifically a *better* homeland. If he had not trusted God to fulfill His promise on that account, Abraham likely would have returned home to Ur or Haran, dismayed and disobedient. But Abraham believed that God's kingdom is a better country, a better home. In short, Abraham knew obedience was worth it. He knew God could be trusted.

5. According to 11:16, why was God not ashamed to be called their God?

These saints weren't the only ones who knew God could be trusted; God knew He could be trusted too. In fact, He had already prepared what they were waiting for! He wasn't ashamed to be called their God because He knew for certain—in the way only an eternal, sovereign, omniscient God can know—that He wouldn't let them down. Their faith would not be wasted.

In this chapter that highlights saints for their faith in God, it's worth noting that His esteem as their God had nothing to do with their faithfulness to Him—it had to do with *His* faithfulness to them.

DAY 3

Hebrews 11:17–22

READ HEBREWS 11:17–22

Review 11:17–19.

When Abraham was seventy-five years old, God promised him descendants that would be as numerous as the stars in the sky. For twenty-five years, Abraham and Sarah waited for a child. Then, finally, when Abraham was one hundred years old and Sarah was ninety, fulfillment came in the form of their son Isaac.

1. What did God ask Abraham to do in Genesis 22:1–2?

What? What a confusing request for God to make.

This story brings up an important point: Faith does not ignore reason, but it sometimes goes beyond it. Abraham could have chosen to disobey God because he didn't understand how this act would fulfill the promise God had made to him. But instead, Abraham basically said, "*I don't get it. But I'm going to believe God's promise* and *obey Him at the same time. And I'm going to trust that somehow this works out in ways I can't see yet.*"

There's no scriptural evidence that anyone had yet been raised from the dead, so his faith was not related to any previous experience. His faith was rooted in *his knowledge of God's character*.

Abraham obeyed in faith, and he became the father of many nations (Genesis 22:3–18).

★ 2. Describe a time when God asked you (or someone you know) to obey in a way that seemed confusing at first. What did God ultimately bring from it?

Review 11:20.

The Hebrews audience knew these names as well as their own. These were their ancestors. The references in this passage would have immediately connected with them. When they encountered the reference to Isaac blessing his adult twin sons (Genesis 27:1–40), they would have known these important details:

A. At first, Isaac tried to act on his own preference instead of obeying God's word.
B. God's word prevailed.
C. Isaac "trembled violently" when he witnessed how God is sovereign over the most chaotic human manipulations.
D. Ultimately, Isaac obeyed, blessing his sons according to God's better plans.

Review 11:21.

This pattern continued with his son Jacob. At birth, Jacob was called "deceiver" (Genesis 25:26).

3. In Genesis 32:24–32, what new name did God give to Jacob? Why?

When Jacob wrestled with God, he came away with a blessing and a limp. Jacob's leaning on his staff to bless Joseph's sons signified a remembrance of God's greatness and His sovereignty over the future—beyond what we can see.

Jacob had seen God work great provision out of confusing circumstances. His beloved son Joseph had been sold into Egyptian slavery by his jealous brothers. Jacob was told Joseph had been killed, and he mourned bitterly. But years later, when Joseph was an adult, he became the second-in-command in all of Egypt. And it happened just in time to save his whole family—including Jacob—from famine and death.

Review 11:22.

Joseph died with faith on his lips. He didn't get to live in the promised land, but he trusted that his offspring would. He was so confident in the promise of God that he essentially said, *"When this happens, don't leave my bones behind—take me with you!"*

4. Read Joshua 24:32 and summarize what happened.

★ 5. Whose story of faith in today's reading—Abraham's, Isaac's, Jacob's, or Joseph's—is most encouraging to you? Why?

DAY 4

Hebrews 11:23–31

READ HEBREWS 11:23–31

Review 11:23–26.

This passage is a sweet reminder of how God goes before us. Our acts of faith plant seeds for future acts of faith. In short, Moses's story didn't start with Moses. His parents did not fear the orders of the king. They saw that God's blessing was on their child, and they acted in faith to preserve his life.

Faith can imbue us with courage, because fear of the Lord dwarfs other fears. While faith is somewhat different from courage, it certainly can enable us to do bold things with God's help (Psalm 27; Habakkuk 3:19). And following in the footsteps of his parents—whom he may not have even remembered—Moses rejected his adopted royal title and its benefits. He chose the harder, humbler path.

★ 1. Have you ever had an experience of humbling yourself or being humbled in preparation for God's better purposes? Describe that experience.

2. According to 11:26, what did Moses experience? Circle the correct answer.

Wealth

The treasures of Egypt

Sharing in the sufferings of Christ

The praise of man

Moses lived some thirteen hundred years (or more) before Jesus was born. But because he chose the path of obedience—and suffered on behalf of God's people, just as Jesus did—he serves as a model for all believers after him, including us.

3. Based on 11:26, is it wrong to seek a reward?

4. Look back at 11:6. What reward do you think Moses was seeking?

Review 11:27–28.

It took faith for Moses to return to Egypt when he knew Pharaoh might kill him. It took faith to believe that lamb's blood on a doorpost would save a household from the Angel of Death. (If you're unfamiliar with the story of Passover, check out Exodus 3–15.) Moses endured as "seeing him who is invisible."

Review 11:29–31.

5. Review the definition of faith from 11:1. Keeping this in mind, describe the difference between faith and courage as it relates to the Israelites and the Egyptians in 11:29.

When the Israelites crossed the flooded Jordan, there was no turning back. God had a promised land for them—and now they had to go claim it. Joshua 1–6 tells the story of Moses's servant Joshua leading the Israelites to victory at the intimidating walled city of Jericho. But the victory came by unconventional means.

God didn't tell them to prepare cannons or sharpen swords. He told them to walk silently around Jericho for six days. And on the seventh day, they were to shout.

★ 6. How do you think the Israelites' faith was impacted as they walked around a city silently for six days while the enemy on the walls watched?

In this story, we see faith is patient, expectant—and not dependent upon human perfection. There might have been others in Jericho with a cleaner record, but it was Rahab the pagan prostitute whom God chose to bring into His story. Though she had not seen God, she believed He exists and rewards those who seek Him (11:6). And by faith, she became one of the five esteemed women listed in the genealogy of Jesus (Matthew 1:5).

DAY 5

Hebrews 11:32–40

READ HEBREWS 11:32–40

Review 11:32–35a.

The original Jewish Christian audience of this book were familiar with all the names in 11:32. So let's catch up with the Hebrews' knowledge and see what thread we notice throughout the stories of these Old Testament saints.

1. Use the passages provided to help you briefly summarize the stories of the people in the table.

Name	Found in . . .	In Unbelief . . .	By Faith . . .
	Judges 6:11–40; 7:2–25	Initially doubted God's word to him and repeatedly asked for confirmation	Mightily used by God to defeat an army so large their camels numbered like sand on the seashore
	Judges 4:4–24	Hesitated when the prophet Deborah brought him the Lord's command	
	Judges 13:1–5; 16:1–21		
	Judges 11:28–40	Made and kept a foolish vow that resulted in his daughter's death	Used by God to defeat the Ammonites

Through each of these figures, God performed mighty deeds—despite their failures, shortcomings, and foolishness. None were perfect, and none would ever be able to attain righteousness by their own merit. They all still needed the ultimate object of their faith—Christ Jesus—for their salvation. They were saved by faith in *His* works, not their own.

King David gets only a passing mention here, but perhaps he's the person on this list you're the most familiar with. His story serves as a reminder of our need for the finished work of Christ to pay our sin debt and reconcile us to the Father.

He was called "a man after [God's] own heart" (1 Samuel 13:14). As a teenager, David defeated the giant Goliath, before whom the entire army of Israel had cowered (1 Samuel 17:4–57). As a young shepherd, David killed both lions and bears with the help of the Lord (1 Samuel 17:36–37). And as an adult, he received victory from God wherever he went (2 Samuel 8:6) and accomplished every item listed in 11:33. And *still*, he sinned egregiously against Uriah and Bathsheba, had tremendous failings with his own children (2 Samuel 11:1–27; 18:33), and in his final words to his son Solomon, issued a death warrant on the head of a man he had promised to pardon (1 Kings 2:8–9).

The prophet Samuel had a similarly complicated story: He served God faithfully, but the same could not be said of his sons (1 Samuel 8:3). This is the beauty of digging deep into the Word of God for understanding. At first glance, Hebrews 11 might have looked like an intimidating list of amazing humans. Upon further inspection, it's actually an invitation to join the list of imperfect people who serve an amazing God.

In 11:33–35a, we see a tidal wave of victories over circumstances by faith. And though no names are mentioned here, the stories listed bring to mind saints the original audience knew well (and perhaps you do too).

2. Match these Hall of Faith snapshots with their Old Testament stories.

Stopped the mouths of lions	Shadrach, Meshach, and Abednego (Daniel 3:26–27)
Quenched the power of fire	Elijah (1 Kings 19:2)
Escaped the edge of the sword	Samuel (1 Samuel 7:10)
Were made strong out of weakness	Daniel (Daniel 6:23)
Put foreign armies to flight	the Shunamite woman (2 Kings 4:8–37)
Received back their dead by resurrection	Esther (Esther 4:14)

There are times, however, when the victories of faith aren't ones where people overcome their circumstances. Instead, their victory is found when faith helps them persevere *despite* their circumstances.

Review 11:35b–38.

The apostle Paul lost many privileges and positions when he became a follower of Jesus. As he reflected on it, he described the things he lost as garbage when compared to knowing Christ (Philippians 3:8). He knew that suffering for Christ was worth it. Like Abraham, he kept eternity in view.

Stephen was stoned to death (Acts 7:54–60). Paul endured everything listed in 11:36. And roughly twenty-five years before this letter was written, King Herod sent orders for James the brother of John to be killed by the sword (Acts 12:1–2). The description of people wearing animal skins and living in caves brings to mind the prophet Elijah—and even John the Baptist, who was beheaded in prison after he called the king to account for his infidelity (Mark 6:17–29).

These stories serve as a stark reminder: Never confuse earthly prosperity for God's delight in and approval of a person. In fact, as Scripture tells us the stories of these saints (and their deaths), it reminds us that *the world was not worthy of them.*

Review 11:39–40.

This final section reiterates the concept we discussed on Day 2:

A. Specific, amazing promises were fulfilled *during* the lifetimes of these saints, and
B. some of these people did not see the new covenant ushered in during their lifetimes (11:13).

But we get to!

The new covenant is here now! And we're a part of this story. How much more reason we have to live by faith! The word *perfect* here carries the meaning "complete" and points to the unity of all God's people, across all time. We live in a single, unified story of redemption through Christ. He's where the joy is!

3. What stood out to you most in this week's study? Why?

★ 4. What did you learn or relearn about God and His character this week?

DAY 6

Corresponding Psalm & Prayer

READ PSALM 18

1. What correlation do you see between Psalm 18 and this week's study?

2. What portions of this psalm stand out to you most?

3. Close by praying this prayer aloud:

Father,

You made Abraham into a great nation. You freed Your people from slavery. You gave them the land You promised. You set apart

David as king. You protected Daniel from the lions. You rescued his friends from the furnace. You raised Esther up as queen. You brought Your people back from exile. And at just the right time, You sent Your Son to save all who will believe in Him. Who is there like You? No one! Your way is perfect and Your Word is true.

I know Your promises are true, God, but in long seasons of waiting, I've doubted You. Like Sarah, I've tried to take my future into my own hands. I know this isn't my home, Lord, but I've acted like it is. I've been preoccupied with worries about things like completing tasks, earning money, and preserving my reputation. I'm sorry, God. I lift my gaze from the things of this world and I fix my eyes on You.

Will You grant me the kind of faith that turns what's unseen into what's seen? If Your plan is for me to overcome my present circumstances, then help me overcome them by faith in You. If Your plan is for me to persevere through my present circumstances, then help me persevere by faith in You. When I need to humble myself like Moses, let my posture come from faith in You. When I need to take bold action like Moses's parents, let my courage come from faith in You. Remind me that it's all because of You, Lord.

You're better than all my best works. May my deeds point to Your faithfulness. I surrender my life to You, Lord—every moment of my day, each decision I make, I yield my will and way to Your perfect will and way.

I love You too. Amen.

DAY 7

Rest, Catch Up, or Dig Deeper

WEEKLY CHALLENGE

On Day 5, we learned that the Hebrews Hall of Fame was an invitation to join in—to imitate their faith! On a sheet of paper, create an artistic representation of your own "by faith" testimony. Don't let the word *artistic* throw you off! This doesn't need to be a masterpiece. This is simply an opportunity to help you see (by creating a visual aid) what God has done in your life.

Here are some helpful tips:

A. Look backward, not forward. Recall how God has already worked faith in your life.

B. If possible, use Scripture as a guide in your testimony of God's faithfulness.

For example, if your name is John, you could write something like this: "By faith, John trusted God no matter what. By faith, John believed God's promises even when the waiting seemed long. By faith, John entrusted his past to God—assured that He who began a good work in John will carry it on to completion until the day of Christ Jesus (Philippians 1:6)."

Keep it in your Bible or journal, or hang it somewhere as a reminder of how far God has brought you!

WEEK 9

Hebrews 12

Scripture to Memorize

For they disciplined us for a short time as it seemed best to them, but he disciplines us for our good, that we may share his holiness.

Hebrews 12:10

DAILY BIBLE READING

Day 1: Hebrews 12:1–2

Day 2: Hebrews 12:3–11

Day 3: Hebrews 12:12–17

Day 4: Hebrews 12:18–24

Day 5: Hebrews 12:25–29

Day 6: Psalm 94

Day 7: Catch-Up Day

Corresponds to Day 357 of *The Bible Recap*.

WEEKLY CHALLENGE

See page 205 for more information.

DAY 1

Hebrews 12:1–2

READ HEBREWS 12:1–2

Review 12:1.

Today's section begins with another *therefore*, instructing us to apply what we've already learned.

The saints listed in Hebrews 11 faced great obstacles in their faith, but they never gave up. This great cloud of witnesses could refer to the list of people we just read about. Or these witnesses could be anyone who has run (or is running) the race with endurance.

★ 1. Who has set a great example of faith for you? (It could be someone you know from a distance or someone close to you. They could be living or with the Lord.) How has their "race" of faith encouraged you?

When you picture this cloud of witnesses, you might picture a stadium filled with the saints who have gone before us, or maybe you picture them watching from heaven, cheering us on. But the meaning is far richer than that.

In this context, the word *witness* actually means "someone who testifies." And what are these saints testifying about? The finished work of Jesus! The legacy of these beloved saints speaks to "the surpassing worth of knowing Christ" (Philippians 3:8).

2. What two things did the writer of Hebrews tell his audience to lay aside?

Some scholars believe the reason the writer used two different words is because he was talking about two different types of hindrances. For this Hebrew audience, he might have been referring to the rules and rituals of the law (weight) that kept them from freely experiencing God's grace. But he also wanted them to lay aside the things that ensnare or entangle them (sin).

3. What are some things, perhaps some good and some bad, that you might need to lay aside to efficiently run the race?

The author used the word *endurance* because the Christian life is a marathon, not a sprint. And it's certainly no walk in the park. In fact, the Greek word for *race* here is *agōn*, which is where we get our English word *agony*. But we're able to endure because we know we run with purpose.

Paul said, "Do you not know that in a race all the runners run, but only one receives the prize? So run that you may obtain it" (1 Corinthians 9:24). Paul knew he wasn't on a hamster wheel or running aimlessly around a track. Paul ran because he knew God is a rewarder of those who diligently seek Him (Hebrews 11:6).

Review 12:2.

It can feel far too easy to compare ourselves to other believers. But we're all running our own race. Maybe you're new to the Christian faith and you're just excited to be in the race at all. Maybe you've been at this for a while and you're completely exhausted, ready to give up. Or maybe you're not even sure where you fit in God's big plan.

4. Circle the illustration that resonates with you in your current season.

This isn't a competition. Instead of looking around and playing the comparison game, Scripture tells us to fix our eyes on Jesus. He's both the founder and perfecter of our faith. We can count on Him to complete the work He started in us (Philippians 1:6), because what God initiates He will sustain and He will fulfill.

★ 5. What are some practical ways you can fix your eyes on Jesus instead of comparing yourself to others? Is there anything you need to add to (or subtract from) your life to help you with this?

Nobody set a better example of endurance than Christ. As we've already seen, He endured pain, humiliation, and a level of suffering we can't comprehend. Why? Because He had His eyes on the prize—and that prize was *our salvation*. What great love!

After enduring the shame and suffering of the cross, Jesus sat down at the right hand of God. Taking His rightful place of victory, He declared that the work is finished.

DAY 2

Hebrews 12:3–11

READ HEBREWS 12:3–11

Review 12:3–4.

Today's study begins by both completing yesterday's thought and introducing the next. Setting our minds on Christ's endurance motivates us to follow His lead and persevere. As we've already learned, the Hebrew believers were starting to feel the heat of persecution. But it wasn't just persecution they struggled against; it was also sin—a struggle every believer can relate to.

1. Do you ever feel discouraged about your struggles with sin? Are there areas where you feel you should have overcome by now?

The writer reminded his audience of Christ's endurance in order to exhort them in their weariness. But he also did this to open their eyes to God's grace and love in relation to discipline.

Review 12:5–9.

2. According to 12:6, who does the Lord discipline?

"The one he ______"

"Every ______ whom he ______"

Note: The Greek word for *son* here, and throughout this passage, simply refers to children or offspring—not strictly males.

3. Who are the *only* people God disciplines? What does it reveal about those He doesn't discipline?

Before we continue, it's crucial to identify what God's discipline is and what it's not. The Greek word for *discipline* here is *paideuō*, which means "to train children" or "to teach." It is not *timoreo*, which refers to punishment or vengeance. As believers, we will never experience the vengeance or wrath of God because Jesus took that on for us at the cross. Isaiah 53:5 is a beautiful reminder: "He was pierced for our transgressions; he was crushed for our iniquities; upon *him* was the *chastisement* that brought us peace, and with his wounds we are healed" (emphasis added).

★ 4. When God has disciplined you, have you viewed it as His anger or His love? Did you feel God was out to get you or out to rescue you?

If you had parents who demonstrated God's love to you in your childhood, you may still recall the sadness or frustration you felt when they disciplined you. In hindsight, you can probably see how it was for your good. If you didn't have parents who showed you godly love and care, this is an opportunity to see how God is a better Father.

If you have children in your life (kids, grandkids, nieces, nephews, students, etc.), you likely understand more about God's heart when He disciplines. Your heart aches when you have to discipline them, but it comes from a heart overflowing with love. You want nothing but the best for them. And the love we feel for the kids in our lives pales in comparison to the love God has for *all* His kids.

★ 5. Can you see the need for God's discipline in your life? Explain.

Discipline from the Father looks different for everyone. Some moments are more painful than others. But through it all, He's still guiding us toward His plan and His best for us.

Review 12:10–11.

6. What two results of God's discipline did the writer describe here?

Talk about a good trade! We may think we enjoy sinning and doing things our own way, but rest assured: God's way is *always* better. He takes our sin and trades it for holiness. He takes our pride and exchanges it for peace. He takes our foolishness and replaces it with righteousness. "Be subject to the Father of spirits and live" (12:9). These are the promises available to us when we yield to Him.

DAY 3

Hebrews 12:12–17

READ HEBREWS 12:12–17

While we don't know who the human writer of Hebrews was, it seems obvious he had an encouraging, discerning heart. He looked around at the family of believers and saw their weariness. Whether from discipline, sin struggles, or persecution, they needed fresh wind in their sails to continue to endure.

Review 12:12–13.

The author painted a vivid picture of the discouragement, fear, and exhaustion that likely plagued his readers. The imagery he used here is pulled directly from Isaiah 35—a passage deeply connected to his readers' Jewish heritage. Isaiah wrote of Israel's return to their homeland after being captured and exiled in enemy territory for seventy years.

In yesterday's study, we read about the discipline of the Lord. It's possible the author's audience was dragging their feet in their pursuit of holiness. If they continued down that path, they simply delayed their healing and growth.

1. Is there an area—past or present—where you know you've delayed your spiritual or emotional healing because you're unwilling to yield to the Lord's discipline? Without listening to God's voice, what is the best outcome you can hope for?

Review 12:14–16a.

Here, the writer addressed what it means to live selflessly in Christian community.

★ 2. List the six commands and warnings the writer gave his audience. Then, in your own words, describe how each can affect the body of believers. One is provided for you.

Command or Warning	Effect on the Body of Believers
Extend the grace of God to everyone	The community of believers lives in harmony and forgives grievances quickly.

Review 12:16b–17.

The writer provides the example of Esau (from Genesis 25:19–34), a story every Jewish person at this time was familiar with. And while the story took place millennia ago, unfortunately it's one that will resonate with most of us today.

Esau and Jacob were twins. Esau was born first; thus, he was granted the birthright. In that culture, the birthright held great legal and social significance, as well as an inheritance from the father.

In a scenario that can only be described as dramatic, Esau came home from an exhausting day and had a conversation with his brother Jacob that went something like this:

Esau: I'm starving! Give me some of that stew!

Jacob: I'll trade you some stew for your entire inheritance.

Esau: An inheritance is worthless to me if I fall over dead right now! And I'll die if I don't get some food!

Jacob: So you'll sell me your birthright if I ladle you some stew?

Esau: Fine! You can have it.

★ 3. What are your thoughts about Esau's decision? Do you think he considered the long-term consequences of this short-term satisfaction?

While this might sound like the most foolish decision in the entire book of Genesis, it serves as a cautionary tale for us all. When 12:17 says Esau "sought [repentance] with tears," the author wasn't referring to a repentant heart that desired to be right with the Lord. God's forgiveness was always available to Esau. Esau simply wanted his birthright back. He wanted to undo the damage he'd done by selling his birthright for a moment of pleasure. He wasn't *repentant*; he was *regretful*—there's a big difference (2 Corinthians 7:10).

For Esau, it was stew. But "stew" can represent any number of things. We trade an opportunity to extend grace for a chance to get the last word in an argument. We swap a chance to represent Christ to the barista for a moment of anger over our latte not being made according to our order. The list goes on.

If we aren't careful to consider the consequences in a heated moment, we'll find ourselves trading our inheritance for a measly bowl of stew, and we can't get those moments back. Thankfully, we serve a gracious and forgiving God. We can't undo the painful consequences of our actions, but we can begin healing as we go to the Father for forgiveness. "If we confess our sins, he is faithful and just to forgive us our sins and purify us from all unrighteousness" (1 John 1:9).

4. Have you been tempted to trade your inheritance for short-term satisfaction? On the bowl of stew below, write a prayer of confession and begin the process of healing.

DAY 4

Hebrews 12:18–24

READ HEBREWS 12:18–24

Many have referred to today's section as "The Tale of Two Mountains." The writer of Hebrews described the best of times and the worst of times. But at its core, this portion of Scripture paints a vivid picture of the peace available to every Christian who rests in God's grace.

Review 12:18–21.

Though the location isn't actually named, the writer began with a description of Mount Sinai—the place where Moses received the law from God when the Israelites were in the wilderness (Exodus 19–34). The writer didn't have to name the mountain because his audience knew exactly what he was talking about.

The Hebrews account closely mirrors the experience Moses wrote about in Exodus. God gave strict instructions about who could and couldn't approach Mount Sinai when God's presence descended to earth. Exodus 19:10 tells us that Moses had to "consecrate" the people before God revealed His glory to them on the mountain.

1. **Using a Bible dictionary, define *consecrate*.**

God is holy, and His people had to be made holy too. Despite their wickedness, God made a way to come down to the nation of Israel so His people might experience His glory. But as the writer of Hebrews described in12:18–21, that was an experience Moses and the Israelites could barely endure.

2. On the mountain below, list Sinai's characteristics.

3. How did the people respond? How did Moses respond?

We might read this and think, *Why is God so mean and terrifying in the Old Testament?* But God isn't mean—He's righteous, just, and holy. And throughout the story, we see Him leaning in with mercy and love to draw near to His people (Exodus 19:6). It was important for His people to understand the incredible "set apartness" of God. God's majesty and holiness is an experience we shouldn't take lightly.

At Mount Sinai, God gave Israel the laws they would need to live by. While these rules purified them for the moment, they didn't create a change of heart.

So God brought them to a different mountain.

Review 12:22–24a.

Zion was a literal place that was closely associated with Jerusalem. This mountain probably looked more like a hill.

4. On the mountain below, write what God's people experience at Mount Zion.

If his Jewish audience was feeling any desire to go back to their old laws and rituals, this served as a vivid reminder of all Christ had delivered them from.

As we saw in 10:14, "by a single offering he has perfected for all time those who are being sanctified." The old covenant required Israel to keep a list of rules to purify themselves. Under the new covenant, they could simply believe in Jesus and receive Him as their Savior to experience His perfect grace and forgiveness. By trusting in Jesus, they weren't made *momentarily* clean—He exchanged their heart of stone for a heart of flesh (Ezekiel 36:26).

★ 5. Do you still find yourself at Mount Sinai, trying to clean yourself up in order to approach God? Or is your relationship with Christ more characterized by Mount Zion, resting in the grace He died to give you?

Living according to Sinai, checking boxes and following rituals, doesn't produce holiness. There is no formula for sanctification. The better choice is Zion. Among other things, the more we simply rest in God's grace—the more we fix our eyes on what He accomplished on our behalf—the more we grow to look like Jesus.

Review 12:24b.

In Hebrews 11, we learned about Abel's faithful sacrifice, which led to his death. Some scholars say Abel's blood refers to the animal sacrifice he presented to God. Others say this refers to Abel's murder, which cried out for vengeance (Genesis 4:10). Regardless, the blood of Jesus "speaks a better word" because it satisfies God's wrath, saves completely (7:25), and testifies of His grace.

DAY 5

Hebrews 12:25–29

READ HEBREWS 12:25–29

Review 12:25.

Yesterday we learned that the blood of Jesus "speaks." When Jesus died for our sins, His blood preached a sermon of grace. Our salvation and sanctification rest on the unmerited grace that was bestowed on us at the cross.

So what hope do we have if we reject this message?

Anytime the law was broken in the Old Testament, the consequences were severe. The Israelites couldn't escape the wrath of God when they refused to follow His ways.

Make no mistake: No one who refuses Jesus will escape God's wrath.

1. Read Matthew 25:41–46. What did Jesus say would be the sentence for those who do not belong to Him?

When we compare God in the Old Testament and Jesus in the New Testament, we might tend to think that God is the bad cop and Jesus is the good cop. At best, this is bad theology—the Father, Son, and Holy Spirit are one. As God in the flesh, Jesus reveals the Father's heart to us (Colossians 1:15).

And at worst, this is an extremely dangerous way of thinking. Showing God's unchanging nature, Jesus spoke about hell more than anyone else in the Bible. Just like the Father did in the Old Testament, Jesus warned people about the consequences of remaining unrepentant.

★ 2. Have you ever held an incorrect view of God's and Jesus's natures? For instance, have you ever seen them as having opposite, or even different natures? How have your views about the Father and the Son changed?

Review 12:26–27.

The quotation in 12:26 comes directly from Haggai 2. The temple had been destroyed because of Israel's disobedience, but through the prophet Haggai, God promised that one day He would shake the nations who had harmed His people. The writer of Hebrews revealed that this prophecy also pointed to an eternal kingdom that will never be shaken.

Picture a child's piece of art made with glitter. First, she squeezes glue onto a piece of paper. While the glue is still wet, she liberally pours glitter all over the paper. Then she carefully pours the excess glitter into a trash can (still managing to leave traces of glitter all over the house for years to come). All that's left after she's shaken off the glitter is what stuck to the glue. The glue kept all the necessary glitter in place, and only what was unnecessary for the completed artwork was removed.

This is a picture of what God's kingdom will be when He shakes the earth "yet once more." All of our worries, materialism, idols, and distractions will be destroyed—all that remains will be what is perfect, right, and good—only what belongs to the Lord. That is the kingdom Jesus has made available to us!

Review 12:28.

★ 3. What should be our response to God's willingness to receive us into His unshakable kingdom? Does this accurately describe your response to your salvation?

What Israel experienced at Mount Sinai was reverence and awe as they looked upon God's glory. Now that we've come to Mount Zion, we stand in awe and reverence because we know what we've been rescued from. Look around: One day, all that's broken will pass away. And if it weren't for Christ, you would be part of that shaking. The only response to His grace and mercy is worship.

4. Read Romans 12:1. How can you live this out on a practical level in your daily life?

Review 12:29.

Believe it or not, this is good news. God's fire is all-consuming—but if you belong to Jesus, God's fire will never consume *you*. When Jesus died in our place, He took on the penalty of sin that should have consumed us. But the fire of God's wrath and justice still roars toward His enemies.

We were once His enemies (Romans 5:10), so now that we've been saved from His wrath, may we live with overflowing joy and gratitude. He's where the joy is!

5. What stood out to you most in this week's study? Why?

6. What did you learn or relearn about God and His character this week?

DAY 6

Corresponding Psalm & Prayer

READ PSALM 94

1. What correlation do you see between Psalm 94 and this week's study?

2. What portions of this psalm stand out to you most?

3. Close by praying this prayer aloud:

Father,

You are righteous, just, and holy—a consuming fire whose kingdom cannot be shaken. You are also forgiving, good, and loving—an eternal reward who gives me everything I need.

I've received Your grace, Lord, but I haven't extended it to others. I've insisted on having the last word. I've been sexually immoral. I've been bitter. And I repent. I lay aside every weight and sin that clings so closely, and I cling to You instead.

When I need discipline from You, help me remember that it's part of Your love. You never forsake Your people, so teach and train me, God. Even if it's painful, help me to know that it's good.

You're better than any earthly prize. May my endurance testify to Your goodness. I surrender my life to You, Lord—every moment of my day, each decision I make, I yield my will and way to Your perfect will and way.

I love You too. Amen.

DAY 7

Rest, Catch Up, or Dig Deeper

WEEKLY CHALLENGE

On Day 1, we read Hebrews 12:1, "Let us also lay aside every weight, and sin which clings so closely, and let us run with endurance the race that is set before us."

Spend a few minutes researching how runners train for a big race. Look up training schedules and nutrition plans. What types of clothes do they wear, and how do they get fitted for shoes? How many days a week do they train?

Make a mental assessment: Compare the discipline of a runner who wants a medal to the way Christians must discipline themselves to live for Christ.

In Day 1's third prompt, you listed things you might need to lay aside to efficiently run the race. This week, make a plan to put that into practice. Begin your new training regimen!

WEEK 10

Hebrews 13

Scripture to Memorize

For the moment all discipline seems painful rather than pleasant, but later it yields the peaceful fruit of righteousness to those who have been trained by it.

Hebrews 12:11

DAILY BIBLE READING

Day 1: Hebrews 13:1–6

Day 2: Hebrews 13:7–13

Day 3: Hebrews 13:14–16

Day 4: Hebrews 13:17–19

Day 5: Hebrews 13:20–25

Day 6: Psalm 118

Day 7: Catch-Up Day

Corresponds to Day 357 of *The Bible Recap.*

WEEKLY CHALLENGE

See page 227 for more information.

DAY 1

Hebrews 13:1–6

READ HEBREWS 13:1–6

Hebrews 12 ended with a call to offer "acceptable worship, with reverence and awe." Continuing that thought, the author challenged the Hebrews to demonstrate this worship through the practical outworking of faith and obedience in their lives.

Review 13:1.

This was a simple command with a wide variety of implications. Familial love among brothers and sisters in Christ is the expectation for everyone who follows Jesus, and it serves as a profound witness to the world (John 13:34–35). The author of Hebrews unpacked some specific examples of what this should look like.

Review 13:2.

1. In the chart on the next page, fill in Example #1 and note why it's important. (You'll fill in the rest of the examples as we go.)

The word *hospitality* means "showing love to strangers." We might associate hospitality with hosting our friends or small group for dinner, or inviting out-of-town relatives to stay with us over the holidays. But for the Hebrew Christians, hospitality meant welcoming strangers—most likely fellow persecuted Christians—into their homes.

Travel was dangerous in the first century, and finding lodging while traveling brought an added challenge. Inns were unruly and unsafe; so for these persecuted Christians to be able to find a welcoming home in a strange city was a godsend.[1]

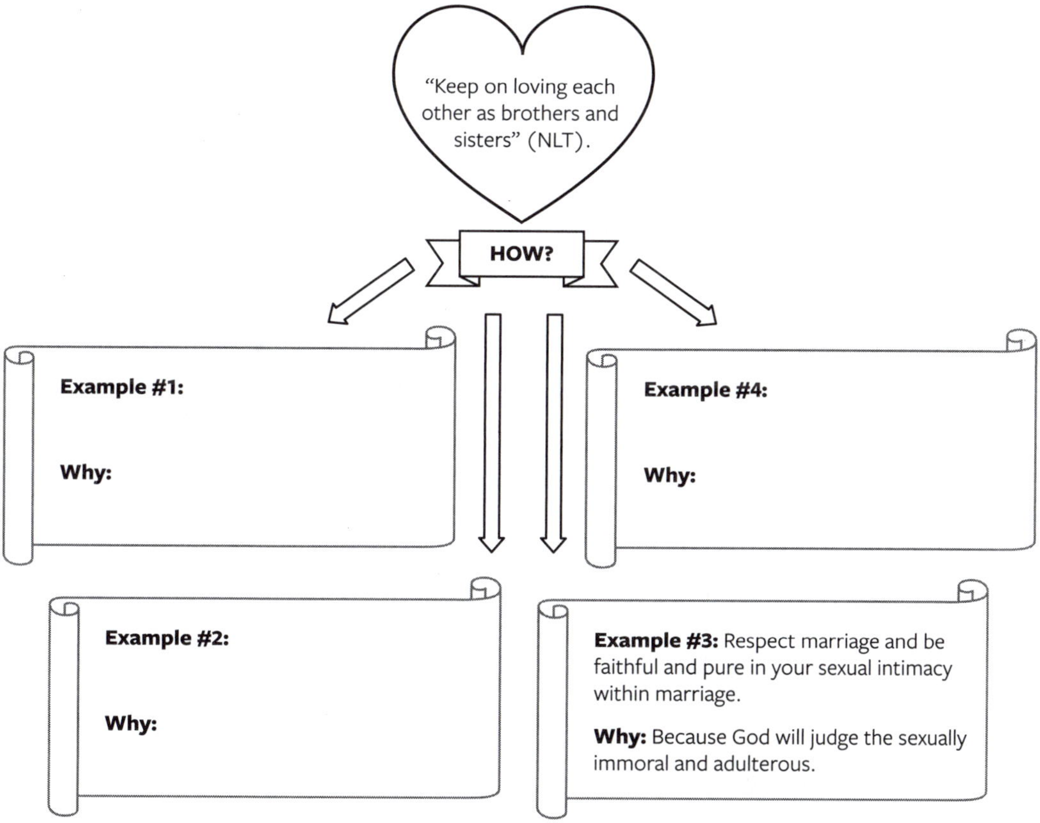

After every command in this section, the author provided the reason why it was important or beneficial. Here, he referenced Abraham, who showed hospitality to angels without even knowing it (Genesis 18:1–8). The author was essentially saying, "*Treat everyone with the honor and respect you would give to an angel. You won't regret it.*"

★ 2. Does this understanding of hospitality change your perspective? Explain. Write down some ways you might show hospitality in your life.

Review 13:3.

3. In the chart above, fill in Example #2 and why it's important.

"Those who are in prison" likely referred to persecuted Christians who were arrested for their faith. And remember what we learned when studying 10:34: Roman prisons didn't provide anything for their inmates—not even the most basic necessities like food or clothing. Prisoners relied solely on the kindness and generosity of others.[2] The author of Hebrews was reminding his readers that their imprisoned brothers and sisters were all a part of the body of Christ—and when one suffered, all suffered (1 Corinthians 12:26).

Review 13:4.

The next example of familial love included two commands. First, respect marriage. And second, be faithful and sexually pure in marriage.

Numerous passages of Scripture command Christians to avoid sexual immorality (1 Corinthians 6:18; 2 Timothy 2:22; 1 Thessalonians 4:3–5). And in this context (marriage), the author of Hebrews specifically commanded faithfulness and purity in sexual intimacy between spouses. Sexual immorality and adultery result from disrespecting this sacred relationship.

Although the author doesn't say how God judges the sexually immoral and adulterous—or what His judgment practically looks like in this area—this was meant to be a strong warning to respect God's commands about sexuality. Regardless of whether His people are married or single, God desires for them to live by faith, demonstrating Christian love, in this area of their lives.

Review 13:5–6.

4. In the chart above, fill in Example #4 and why it's important.

As we learned in 10:34, some Hebrew Christians had lost property and wealth due to persecution.[3] It's also possible that some of the recipients of this letter were more motivated by greed than by love for others. Regardless, the author was encouraging the Hebrews to practice contentment in their financial situations, relying on God as their helper and the one who would never leave them.

★ 5. Place an X on the scale below marking where you are. Or if none of these accurately describes you, feel free to write your own statement.

I love money more than God and people.

I think about money a lot and feel burdened because I don't think I have enough.

I am moving toward contentment but still feel the desire for more.

I am content with what I have.

DAY 2

Hebrews 13:7–13

READ HEBREWS 13:7–13

Review 13:7.

Throughout Scripture, God's people are encouraged to *remember*. Most often, this command is focused on remembering *God*—recalling who He is and what He's done for His people. But sometimes God's people are encouraged to remember brothers and sisters whose lives were examples of faithfulness to Him.

1. Summarize the answers from the text.

Who were the Hebrews supposed to remember?	
What had these people done for the Hebrews?	
What two things were the Hebrews supposed to do as they reflected on these individuals?	

★ 2. Consider your own life. Write down one or two leaders who impacted your relationship with God and include some specific examples of how you saw them trust Him. How have their lives encouraged you to remain faithful to God no matter what? Explain.

Review 13:8–9.

Verse 8 might seem out of place at first, but it's an important bridge between 13:7 and 13:9. The Hebrews' previous leaders had faithfully taught them about Jesus—and Jesus never changes. Praise God! So it was important for the Hebrews to hold fast to the unchanging truth they had learned about Jesus rather than be influenced by other teachings.

Scholars aren't sure what these "diverse and strange teachings" were, but they could have been ascetic practices, Jewish ceremonial meal practices, or ritual observances of some kind.[1] Because the author mentioned foods, it seems likely these teachings involved some kind of food ritual. Regardless of the content of these teachings, the Hebrew Christians should avoid them and remember it was God's grace—not food—that gave them daily strength.

3. Does one of these views make more sense to you than the others? If so, which one and why?

Review 13:10.

Although Christians no longer participated in the sacrificial system at the temple, the author reminded them they still had an altar. Scholars are divided again on what this *altar* referred to, but it could be Communion/ Eucharist (the Lord's Supper), Christian Passover feasts, the altar in the heavenly sanctuary, or Christ's sacrificial death (His atonement). Regardless of the specifics, all of these options ultimately point to Jesus's sacrifice, which is where the author directed the Hebrews.

4. Does one of these views make more sense to you than the others? If so, which one and why?

Review 13:11–13.

In the same way the sacrificial animals' bodies were taken outside the camp in Leviticus 16:27, Jesus Himself—the ultimate, perfect sacrifice—was crucified outside the city walls of Jerusalem.

5. **Look up *sanctify* (13:12) in a Greek lexicon and circle what it means below.**[2]

A. To separate from profane things and dedicate to God (i.e., dedicate people to God)
B. To purify by expiation: free from the guilt of sin
C. Both A and B
D. To make perfect
E. All of the above

Jesus's sacrifice sanctified us: It removed the guilt of sin *and* consecrated us unto God. It brought us into relationship with Him—to share in His life and His suffering. The author encouraged the Hebrews to not only accept the gift of salvation brought about by Jesus's suffering, but join Him in suffering outside the camp.

Jesus's suffering included intense physical agony during the crucifixion, as well as humiliation, shame, and disgrace. Through it all, Jesus remained faithful and endured to the end. The author was calling the Hebrews—and us—to join Jesus by faithfully bearing* the same reproach (disgrace) He did.

* This passage is not speaking to scenarios of domestic abuse. If you are in an unsafe environment, please seek safety and wise counsel.

★ 6. Consider the call to join Jesus "outside the camp." What might this look like in your life?

DAY 3

Hebrews 13:14–16

READ HEBREWS 13:14–16

Review 13:14.

The author knew bearing the shame and reproach experienced by Jesus would seem difficult—or even impossible—if the Hebrews didn't remember an important eternal truth.

1. Write the first half of 13:14 next to the earthly city in the image below. Then, write the second half of the verse next to the heavenly city.

Throughout this letter, the Hebrews were repeatedly encouraged by the reality that Jesus is better. He's better than angels, Moses, the priesthood, Melchizedek, and any sacrifice ever offered. Because He's better, He was worthy of the Hebrews' faithfulness. And they could be encouraged to remain steadfast by remembering the lasting hope of a better city, prepared for them by God (11:10).

Although the Hebrews were likely experiencing persecution and other trials, the author reminded them of the future reality of rest that God had promised them. This truth would help them fight the temptation to return to the alleged safety of Judaism to protect themselves from persecution.

2. Read Revelation 21:1–4. Where is the heavenly city? How is it described?

Review 13:15.

Just as the author previously assured the Hebrews that they still had an altar, here he highlighted the sacrifices they'd continue to present to God—sacrifices of praise.

★ 3. **Look up this verse in the NLT and NIV.** How do these translations help you better understand what it means to "acknowledge his name"? Why would this have been important for the Hebrews? What does this mean in your life?

Review 13:16.

On Day 1, we saw how Christian worship was expressed through brotherly (familial) love. Here, the author provided another example of love for the Hebrews to follow: Do good and share with others. This was another new covenant sacrifice that was pleasing to God.

Sharing with others might make you think about two children being encouraged to share their toys. And while that's a good starting place, the concept is far richer.

4. **Look up *sharing* (13:16) in a Greek lexicon and write the definition below.**

This kind of sharing came from a place of deep love and fellowship within the body of Christ. The Hebrews were instructed to give to those in need—not out of duty, but because they were family! The close connection between brothers and sisters in Christ would be evident in their willingness to share with each other.

In 13:5, the Hebrews had been warned to steer clear of the love of money. This call to do good and embrace sacrificial giving might have also been a practical way for them to fight against greed and seek contentment.

★ 5. What connection do you see between giving and sacrifice? How might you apply this in your own life?

DAY 4

Hebrews 13:17–19

READ HEBREWS 13:17–19

Review 13:17a.

Following the pattern we've seen throughout Hebrews 13, the author gave two commands and explained their importance.

1. Fill in the chart below.

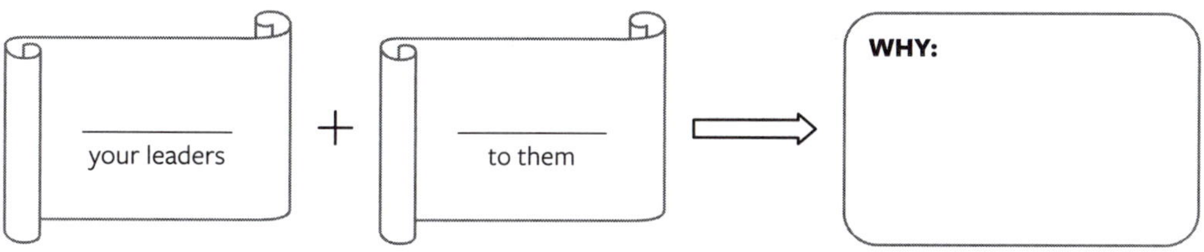

The author mentioned leaders back in 13:7, but it's likely he had two different groups in mind. The leaders in 13:7 had shared the gospel with the Hebrews, and might have started the Hebrew church (or churches), but weren't the current leaders. This second group were those tasked with leading the Hebrews when the author wrote his epistle.

Leadership in the early church generally consisted of both elders (shepherd-teachers) and deacons (servant-ministers). Deacons served the churches mainly in practical ways like administration, serving the poor and sick in the church, and managing giving (Acts 6:1–6). Elders were responsible for "shepherding the flock," which included teaching, leading, and caring for the spiritual well-being of the church (Acts 20:28; 1 Peter

5:1–4; James 5:14). The author likely had elders in mind because they oversaw the church's spiritual health.

Church leadership is a weighty task. Godly character is paramount in these roles, and Scripture encourages the local church to uphold these high standards (1 Timothy 3:1–13). The author reminded the Hebrews that their leaders would give an account for *how* they had led. So the implication is that church leaders will give this account to Jesus, the chief shepherd.

Review 13:17b.

The author was encouraging the Hebrews to make their leaders' jobs as easy as possible. There was no need to add difficulty to an already weighty and burdensome task. Obeying and yielding to their *godly* leaders would allow those leaders to serve the Hebrews with joy instead of grief.

In short, *"Be easy to lead, Hebrews. Be teachable and humble, and avoid grumbling or complaining—this will produce joy in your leaders and help them better care for the spiritual health of the church."* (And who wouldn't prefer to be led by a joyful person?)

★ 2. What do you think makes someone easy to lead? What makes them hard to lead?

3. Would you consider yourself a joy to lead? Why or why not?

Review 13:18–19.

Here, we see a small glimpse into the human author of Hebrews. Being a leader himself, his heart of humility and desire for integrity shone through. He treasured the Hebrews' prayers that he would continue leading faithfully—keeping his conscience clear and living honorably.

4. Why did the author urge the Hebrews to pray for him?

Don't miss this. The author was confident that the Hebrews' prayers would make a difference in his life. He trusted that God would move on his behalf, through their prayers, and allow him to visit them soon. The author believed God heard and responded to the prayers of His people.

★ 5. Circle all the statements that correspond with your view of prayer. Optional: Write your own in the space provided.

A. I don't always know how to pray.

B. I think God hears me, but I don't feel like He responds.

C. I know God listens to other people's prayers.

D. I believe prayer makes a difference in my life.

E. I'm confident God hears my prayers and responds to them.

F. I believe prayer makes a difference in the world around me.

G.

Hebrews 13:20–25

READ HEBREWS 13:20–25

Review 13:20–21.

Most New Testament letters close with a benediction (blessing), and the author of Hebrews followed this familiar pattern. His blessing pointed back to many of the themes we've seen throughout this letter in two beautiful and theologically robust verses.

These verses might feel dense, so let's make sure we get the main point of the benediction. The author blessed the Hebrews by saying, *"May God equip you with everything good."*

1. Write the descriptions of God the Father and Jesus in your own words. Fill in the reason God equips His people.

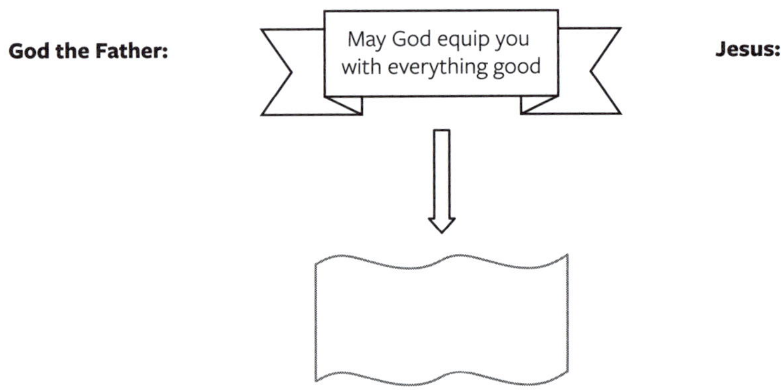

God saves His people *and* He equips His people. God provides His kids with everything good so they can do His will. God Himself is the one working in us so we know Him, follow Him, obey Him, and do the good works He prepared beforehand for us (Philippians 1:6; Ephesians 2:10). He does the doing!

★ 2. Are you encouraged by the reality that God equips you in this way? Explain.

3. What themes or key words do you see repeated in this benediction?

Review 13:22–23.

Even if this exhortation didn't always feel brief, the author of Hebrews packed a lot into thirteen chapters. He closed with a few quick greetings.

Timothy might be a familiar name to you. He was one of Paul's travel companions and served the church in Ephesus for a while (Acts 16:1–5; 1 Timothy 1:3). At some point, he spent time in prison for his faith and apparently had recently been released. It's likely Timothy was closely acquainted with the author.

Review 13:24.

There are two options for who these Italians might be. In AD 49–50, the Roman emperor Claudius forced all Jews to leave Italy. (This was the reason Priscilla and Aquila, two of Paul's ministry partners, were living in Corinth. See Acts 18:1–2.) So it's possible "those who come from Italy" were Jewish Christians who had been kicked out of Italy years before.

Another option is that the author was writing *from* Italy, so he was just saying hi from the Christians who were there with him.[1]

Review 13:25.

The author of Hebrews presented a logical argument from start to finish on the superiority of Jesus—He's the better messenger, the better Moses, the better high priest, the better sacrifice, and the assurance of a better covenant. The invitation of the new covenant—salvation through Christ—is a free gift of grace.

Grace saved the Hebrew believers. And grace would strengthen them in their resolve to persevere by faith. Praise God, the same is true for us! He's where the joy is!

4. What stood out to you most in this week's study? Why?

★ 5. What did you learn or relearn about God and His character this week?

DAY 6

Corresponding Psalm & Prayer

READ PSALM 118

1. What correlation do you see between Psalm 118 and this week's study?

2. What portions of this psalm stand out to you most?

3. Close by praying this prayer aloud:

Father,

You are my God, You are good, and I will give thanks to You! Along with Israel and the house of Aaron and all those who fear You, I say, "Your steadfast love endures forever!"

You have set me free, but I put myself in a cage made of my own sin. You are on my side, but I fear that following You will mean losing money or popularity. You have made me part of Your family, but I haven't loved my brothers and sisters as I should. Forgive me, Lord.

I want You to work in me whatever is pleasing to You. I want to do Your will. I want to bring You glory. So like You did for the Hebrews, will You equip me with everything good?

You're better than every other sacrifice. May all that I am praise Your holy name. I surrender my life to You, Lord—every moment of my day, each decision I make, I yield my will and way to Your perfect will and way.

I love You too. Amen.

DAY 7

Rest, Catch Up, or Dig Deeper

WEEKLY CHALLENGE

On Day 2, we learned about the leaders who influenced the Hebrew Christians. And under Day 2's second prompt, you wrote down one or two leaders who impacted your life.

Write a note to one (or both) of these leaders thanking them for encouraging you. Be sure to include what you've seen in their life that inspires you to imitate their faith. If they're already with the Lord, consider contacting one of their relatives to tell them about the influence their loved one had on your life.

FOR GROUP LEADERS

Thank you for using this study and leading others through it as well! Each week has a wide variety of content (daily Bible reading, content and questions, Scripture memorization, weekly challenge, and resources) to help the reader develop a range of spiritual disciplines. Feel free to include as much or as little of that in your meetings as you'd like. The details provided in How to Use This Study (pp. 7–9) will be helpful to you and all your group members, so be sure to review that information together!

It's up to you and your group how you'd like to structure your meetings, but we suggest including time for discussion of the week's study and Bible text, mutual encouragement, and prayer. You may also want to practice your Scripture memory verses together as a group or in pairs. As you share with each other, "consider how to stir up one another to love and good works" (Hebrews 10:24) and "encourage one another and build one another up" (1 Thessalonians 5:11).

Here are some sample questions to help facilitate discussion. This is structured as a weekly study, but if your group meets at a different frequency, you may wish to adjust the questions accordingly. Cover as many questions as time allows, or feel free to come up with your own. And don't forget to check out the additional resources we've linked for you at MyDGroup.org/Hebrews.

Sample Discussion Questions

What questions did this week's study or Bible text bring up for you?

What stood out to you in this week's study?

What did you notice about God and His character?

How were you challenged by your study of the Bible text? Is there anything you want to change in light of what you learned?

How does what you learned about God affect the way you live in community?

What correlation did you see between the psalm from Day 6 and this week's study of Hebrews?

Have you felt God working in you through the weekly challenge? If so, how?

Is your love for God's Word increasing as we go through this study? If so, how?

Did anything you learned increase your joy in knowing Jesus?

ACKNOWLEDGMENTS

Laura Buchelt, Emily Pickell, Abbey Dane, Emma Dotter, Kirsten McCloskey, and Liz Suggs—thank you for your incredible research, creativity, wisdom, humility, and laughter. I love getting to study God's Word with you! *NO NOTES!*

Emily Watkins—for making sure we stay hydrated!

Lisa Jackson—you continue to be such a gift as a guide, agent, and friend.

And to the rest of the incredible D-Group Team—Rachel Mantooth, Lindsay Ruhter, Warwick Fuller, Jane Long, Meg Mitchell, Evaline Asmah, and our board, leaders, members, and church partners around the world—I love being on mission with you!

NOTES

Week 1: Day 1

1. "English Explanation of Mishnah Sanhedrin 4:3," Sefaria Library, https://www.sefaria.org/English_Explanation_of_Mishnah_Sanhedrin.4.3.1.

Week 1: Day 3

1. D.A. Carson, *For the Love of God: A Daily Companion for Discovering the Treasures of God's Word*, vol. 2 (Crossway, 1999), 50.

Week 1: Day 4

1. "G5048—*teleioō*—Strong's Greek Lexicon (ESV)," Blue Letter Bible, https://www.blueletterbible.org/lexicon/g5048/esv/mgnt/rl0/0-1.

Week 3: Day 3

1. Tremper Longman III and David E. Garland, eds., *The Expositor's Bible Commentary: Hebrews–Revelation*, rev. ed., vol. 13 (Zondervan, 2006), 81–82; "Hebrews 6—A Warning to Discouraged Believers," Enduring Word, https://enduringword.com/bible-commentary/hebrews-6/.

2. John D. Barry et al., *Faithlife Study Bible* (Bellingham, WA: Lexham Press, 2012, 2016), Hebrews 6:7–8.

Week 3: Day 5

1. John D. Barry et al., *Faithlife Study Bible* (Lexham Press, 2012, 2016), note on Hebrews 6:16.

2. "My Hope Is Built on Nothing Less," Edward Mote, 1834, https://hymnary.org/text/my_hope_is_built_on_nothing_less.

Week 4: Day 2

1. Thomas L. Constable, "Notes on Hebrews 2026 Edition," Sonic Light, https://soniclight.com/tcon/notes/html/hebrews/hebrews.htm.

Week 7: Day 3

1. Charles Haddon Spurgeon, "Holding Fast Our Profession," The Spurgeon Center, https://www.spurgeon.org/resource-library/sermons/holding-fast-our-profession/#flipbook/.

Week 7: Day 5

1. John D. Barry et al., *Faithlife Study Bible* (Lexham Press, 2012, 2016), note on Hebrews 10:34.

2. Thomas L. Constable, "Notes on Hebrews 2026 Edition," Sonic Light, https://soniclight.com/tcon/notes/html/hebrews/hebrews.htm.

Week 8: Day 1

1. "Creation Out of Nothing," Theopedia, https://theopedia.com/creation-ex-nihilo.

Week 10: Day 1

1. David L. Allen, *The New American Commentary: An Exegetical and Theological Exposition of Holy Scripture: Hebrews* (B & H Publishing Group, 2010), 607.
2. Thomas L. Constable, "Notes on Hebrews 2026 Edition," Sonic Light, https://soniclight.com/tcon/notes/html/hebrews/hebrews.htm.
3. Constable, "Notes on Hebrews 2026 Edition."

Week 10: Day 2

1. David L. Allen, *Hebrews, The New American Commentary* (B & H Publishing Group, 2010), 614; Donald Guthrie, *Hebrews: An Introduction and Commentary*, vol. 15, Tyndale New Testament Commentaries (InterVarsity Press, 1983), 273.
2. Answer quoted from "G37—*hagiazō*—Strong's Greek Lexicon (ESV)," Blue Letter Bible, accessed April 14, 2026, https://www.blueletterbible.org/lexicon/g37/esv/mgnt/0-1/.

Week 10: Day 5

1. Thomas L. Constable, "Notes on Hebrews 2026 Edition," Sonic Light, https://soniclight.com/tcon/notes/html/hebrews/hebrews.htm.

ABOUT THE EDITOR

TARA-LEIGH COBBLE'S zeal for biblical literacy is at the heart of everything she creates. Her goal is to help people read, understand, and love the Bible. Her daily podcast, *The Bible Recap*, guides listeners through a chronological one-year reading plan. The podcast has over 500 million downloads and reached number one on the Apple Podcast charts in All Categories. She created and leads D-Group International, which has grown into an international network of more than 500 weekly Bible studies that meet in homes, in churches, and online. A *Wall Street Journal* bestselling author, she also writes and hosts a daily radio feature called *The God Shot*, and leads trips to Israel to study the Bible on-site. Tara-Leigh lives in Dallas, Texas, where she has no pets, children, or anything else that might die if she forgets to feed it.

For more information: TaraLeighCobble.com | TheBibleRecap.com | MyDGroup.org | Israelux.com
Social media: @taraleighcobble | @thebiblerecap | @mydgroup | @israeluxtours

MINISTRIES

THE BIBLE RECAP—*READ THE BIBLE*

Est. 2019 | TheBibleRecap.com
Have you ever closed your Bible and thought, *What did I just read?* In about eight minutes a day, our summary walks you through the one-year chronological plan. Available in podcast, YouTube, and book form. Other supplemental resources available for adults and children.

D-GROUP INTERNATIONAL—*STUDY THE BIBLE*

Est. 2009 | MyDGroup.org
Men's and women's Bible study groups that meet weekly—in homes, online, and in churches around the world. D-Groups work through a series of forty studies that cover the entire Bible over the course of a decade.

ISRAELUX—*EXPERIENCE THE BIBLE*

Est. 2014 | Israelux.com
Offering a deluxe tour, incredible dining experiences, luxury accommodations, and life-changing teaching at biblical sites. The beauty of Israel is also captured in TLC's book *Israel: Beauty, Light, and Luxury*, a *Wall Street Journal* bestseller.